T0144451

Image Processing and Machine Learning, Volume 1

Image processing and machine learning are used in conjunction to analyze and understand images. Where image processing is used to pre-process images using techniques such as filtering, segmentation, and feature extraction, machine learning algorithms are used to interpret the processed data through classification, clustering, and object detection. This book serves as a textbook for students and instructors of image processing, covering the theoretical foundations and practical applications of some of the most prevalent image processing methods and approaches.

Divided into two volumes, this first installment explores the fundamental concepts and techniques in image processing, starting with pixel operations and their properties and exploring spatial filtering, edge detection, image segmentation, corner detection, and geometric transformations. It provides a solid foundation for readers interested in understanding the core principles and practical applications of image processing, establishing the essential groundwork necessary for further explorations covered in Volume 2.

Written with instructors and students of image processing in mind, this book's intuitive organization also contains appeal for app developers and engineers.

Image Processing and Machine Learning, Volume 1

Foundations of Image Processing

Erik Cuevas and Alma Nayeli Rodríguez

CRC Press
Taylor & Francis Group
Boca Raton London New York

CRC Press is an imprint of the
Taylor & Francis Group, an **informa** business
A CHAPMAN & HALL BOOK

First edition published 2024
by CRC Press
2385 NW Executive Center Drive, Suite 320, Boca Raton FL 33431

and by CRC Press
4 Park Square, Milton Park, Abingdon, Oxon, OX14 4RN

CRC Press is an imprint of Taylor & Francis Group, LLC

ISBN: 978-1-032-23458-8 (hbk)
ISBN: 978-1-032-26260-4 (pbk)
ISBN: 978-1-003-28741-4 (ebk)

DOI: 10.1201/9781003287414

Typeset in Palatino
by codeMantra

Contents

Preface Volume 1

Image processing is an important area of research because it enables the improvement and manipulation of images for various applications, such as medical imaging, wherein it plays a crucial role in the analysis and diagnosis of X-rays, CT scans, and MRI images. Image processing algorithms can be used in surveillance systems to detect and track objects, enhance image quality, and perform facial recognition. In remote sensing, image processing techniques are used to analyze satellite and aerial images for various purposes such as environmental monitoring and resource management. In multimedia, it is used in applications to enhance and manipulate images for display, such as in photo editing software and video games. Overall, image processing has a wide range of applications and has become a critical tool in many industries, making it an important area of study and research.

Machine learning (ML) is a research field part of artificial intelligence that allows to learn from data and make predictions or decisions without being explicitly programmed. Some of the main applications of ML include automation, where ML algorithms can automate tasks that would otherwise require human intervention, reducing errors and increasing efficiency. In predictive analytics, ML models can analyze large amounts of data to identify patterns and make predictions, which can be used in various applications such as stock market analysis, fraud detection, and customer behavior analysis. In decision-making, ML algorithms can help organizations make better and more informed decisions by providing insights and recommendations based on data.

The combination of image processing and ML involves the use of techniques from both fields to analyze and understand images. Image processing techniques are used to pre-process the images, such as filtering, segmentation, and feature extraction, while ML algorithms are used to analyze and interpret the processed data such as classification, clustering, and object detection. The goal is to use the strengths of each field to build computer vision systems that can automatically understand and analyze images without human intervention. With this combination, image processing techniques can enhance the quality of the images, which improves the performance of ML algorithms. On the other hand, ML algorithms can automatically analyze and interpret images, which reduces the need for manual intervention.

Our primary objective was to create a comprehensive textbook that serves as an invaluable resource for an image processing class. With this goal in mind, we carefully crafted a book that encompasses both the theoretical foundations and practical applications of the most prevalent image processing methods. From pixel operations to geometric transformations, spatial

filtering to image segmentation, and edge detection to color image processing, we have meticulously covered a wide range of topics essential to understanding and working with images. Moreover, recognizing the increasing
relevance of ML in image processing, we have incorporated fundamental ML
concepts and their applications in this field. By introducing readers to these
concepts, we aim to equip them with the necessary knowledge to leverage
ML techniques for various image processing tasks. Our ultimate aspiration is
for this book to be a valuable companion for students and practitioners alike,
providing them with a solid understanding of image processing fundamentals and empowering them to apply these techniques in real-world scenarios.

To cover all the important information, the inclusion of numerous chapters and programs is necessary. Consequently, the resulting book contained
a substantial amount of content and programming examples. However, recognizing that a single-volume book with a multitude of chapters and programs can be overwhelming for readers, the decision to divide the book into
two volumes was made. This division was undertaken with the primary
objective of ensuring that the book was appropriately handled and comprehended by readers. The book becomes more approachable and manageable
by splitting the material into two volumes, preventing readers from feeling
overwhelmed by the sheer volume of the information. This thoughtful division facilitates a smoother learning experience, allowing readers to navigate
through the content more effectively, delve deeper into the material, and
absorb concepts and techniques at their own pace. Ultimately, the decision to
divide the book into two volumes serves the purpose of optimizing readers'
understanding and engagement with the extensive materials and programs
presented within its pages.

With the objective of ensuring that the book can be effectively navigated
and comprehended by readers, we have made the decision to divide it into
two volumes. Volume 1: "Foundations of Image Processing" and Volume 2:
"Advanced Topics in Image Analysis and Machine Learning".

Volume 1 covers the fundamental concepts and techniques in image
processing, starting with pixel operations and their properties and exploring spatial filtering, edge detection, image segmentation, corner detection,
and geometric transformations. It provides a solid foundation for readers
interested in understanding the core principles and practical applications
of image processing. By focusing on these initial six chapters, the volume
establishes the essential groundwork necessary for further exploration in the
field. Building upon the knowledge gained from Volume 1, Volume 2 considers more advanced topics in image analysis. It covers a range of subjects,
including morphological filters, color image processing, image matching,
feature-based segmentation using the mean-shift algorithm, and finally, the
application of singular value decomposition (SVD) for image compression.
In addition to covering the advanced concepts and techniques of image processing, Volume 2 provides several important ML techniques as applied to
the field. Recognizing the increasing significance of ML in image analysis

and understanding its potential for enhancing image processing tasks, we have incorporated relevant ML approaches throughout Volume 2.

The division into two volumes was aimed at ensuring that each volume could stand alone as a self-contained resource. This means that readers have the flexibility to review and study each volume independently, without necessarily relying on the other volume for context or understanding. By maintaining a self-contained structure, readers can approach the material in a modular manner, focusing on specific aspects or revisiting specific chapters as needed.

Welcome to Volume 1 of our book. This volume serves as an introduction to the fundamental concepts and techniques in image processing. It lays the groundwork for understanding the core principles and practical applications of image processing. By focusing on these fundamental topics, Volume 1 aims to provide readers with a solid understanding of the core concepts and techniques in image processing. It forms the basis upon which you can further explore advanced topics and ML applications in Volume 2. Whether you are a student or a practitioner in the field, this volume will equip you with the necessary knowledge to approach image processing tasks with confidence and understanding.

Many books on image processing techniques are geared toward readers with a strong mathematical background. Upon reviewing various related books, the authors noticed the need for a more general and less technical approach to these topics to attract a wider audience of readers and students. This book includes all the topics found in other similar books, but with a greater emphasis on explaining, putting into practice, and utilizing the methods, and less emphasis on the mathematical details.

This book not only covers the key concepts and techniques of image processing but also provides a substantial amount of code and implementations. The authors view this as an important aspect of the book. Even those readers with strong mathematical abilities can struggle to fully grasp a particular approach until they see it in code. By implementing algorithms and methods in code, any confusion or uncertainty is removed, making the material easier to understand and transmit. With this approach, as the reader progresses through the book from simpler to more advanced methods, the focus on computation (the implemented code) allows them to see the various models and reinforce their mathematical understanding.

Many comparable books only focus on the theoretical aspect, while those that cover practical implementations usually present a general approach to developing algorithms from scratch. Our teaching experience has shown that students understand the material faster when they have access to code that they can modify and experiment with. This book uses MATLAB® as the programming language to implement the systems, due to its popularity among engineers and its extensive library collection for various disciplines. Other programming languages such as Java, R, C++, and Python are also used in engineering, but MATLAB stands out for its distinctive features.

For beginner readers, the numerous computational methods used in image processing can be overwhelming due to the vast number of mathematical concepts and techniques involved. Some practical books attempt to address this issue by offering chapters on how to use pre-existing recipes. However, what if the assumptions of the problem are not met? In such cases, it becomes necessary to modify or adapt the algorithm. To accomplish this, it's crucial that the book provides the conceptual understanding needed to appreciate and comprehend the underlying mathematics. The aim of this book is to strike a balance by offering a comprehensive yet accessible view of the most commonly used computational algorithms and popular image processing approaches, with a focus on rigor.

Despite the heavy mathematical concepts involved in image processing methods, it is possible to utilize these models without a deep understanding of their mathematical foundations. For many readers, learning image processing through programming instead of a complex mathematical model is a more feasible goal. This book aims to fulfill this objective.

The teaching of image processing can be effective by blending theoretical knowledge with hands-on computer exercises, allowing students to write their own code for processing image data. As image processing principles are widely used in various fields, such as ML and data analysis, there is a growing demand for engineers who are proficient in these concepts. Many universities respond to this need by offering comprehensive courses in image processing that cover the most widely used techniques. Image processing is perceived as a highly practical subject, inspiring students to see how image transformations can be transformed into code to produce visually appealing effects.

The material has been compiled from a teaching perspective. For this reason, the book is primarily intended as a textbook for undergraduate and postgraduate students of Science, Electrical Engineering, or Computational Mathematics. It is appropriate for courses such as image processing, computer vision, artificial vision, advanced methods, and image understanding. The book was conceived as a complete course that can be covered in a semester.

Volume 1 is organized in a way that allows readers to easily understand the goal of each chapter and reinforce their understanding through practical exercises using MATLAB programs. It consists of six chapters; the details of each chapter are described below.

Chapter 1 explores pixel operations, their properties, and how they are applied in image processing. It also explains the relationship between image histograms and pixel operations and includes numerical examples using MATLAB to help illustrate the concepts.

Chapter 2 focuses on the analysis of spatial filtering, which involves modifying each pixel of an image by considering not only its original value but also the values of its neighboring elements.

In **Chapter 3**, the concepts of the edges or contours of an image are described, which corresponds to an important component for image analysis. The main existing methods for locating edges, their properties, and particularities, which are implemented in MATLAB for the reader's understanding, are also addressed.

Chapter 4 covers the topic of image segmentation and the treatment of binary images. Segmentation involves isolating each individual binary object in an image. After isolating these objects, various properties such as the number of objects, their position, and the number of pixels that make up the object can be evaluated.

Chapter 5 outlines the main methods for identifying corners, their key properties, defining equations, and implementation in MATLAB.

In **Chapter 6**, the primary methods for detecting geometric shapes, such as lines or circles, are covered.

Over a span of more than 5 years, we conducted extensive testing and experimentation to effectively present this material to diverse audiences. Furthermore, we are deeply grateful for the unwavering support and tolerance we received from our students, particularly those from the CUCEI at the University of Guadalajara, Mexico. The invaluable collaborations, assistance, and discussions with our colleagues throughout this journey could fill an additional chapter. We extend our sincerest gratitude to all those who have contributed to this endeavor.

Erik Cuevas
Alma Nayeli Rodriguez
Guadalajara, Jalisco, Mexico

1

Pixel Operations

1.1 Introduction

Pixel operations refer to those operations performed on images where only the pixel value of interest $p = I(x,y)$ from the image is considered [1]. Each new pixel value calculated $p' = I'(x,y)$ is dependent on the value of the original pixel $p = I(x,y)$ at the same position. Thus, it is independent of the values of other pixels, such as its closest neighbors. The new pixel value is determined through a function $f\big[I(x,y)\big]$, so that:

$$f\big[I(x,y)\big] \rightarrow I'(x,y) \tag{1.1}$$

Figure 1.1 shows a representation of this type of operation. If, as in the previous case, the function $f(\cdot)$ is independent of the image coordinates, its values do not depend on the pixel position, so the function is called homogeneous. Examples of typical homogeneous operations are:

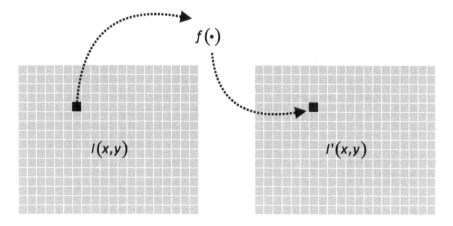

FIGURE 1.1
Representation of pixel operations, in which the resulting pixel depends only on the value of the function operating on the original pixel.

DOI: 10.1201/9781003287414-1

- Contrast and illumination changes in the image
- Application of certain illumination curves
- Inverting or complementing an image
- Threshold segmentation of an image
- Gamma correction of an image
- The color transformation of an image

On the other hand, non-homogeneous pixel operations consider not only the value of the pixel in question but also its relative position in the image, that is $I'(x,y)$.

$$g[I(x,y),x,y] \rightarrow I'(x,y) \qquad (1.2)$$

A frequent operation performed on images using non-homogeneous operations is the changing of contrast or illumination of an image depending on the position of the pixel in the image. Under such conditions, some image pixels will be strongly altered, while other elements will present only small effects.

1.2 Changing the Pixel Intensity Value

1.2.1 Contrast and Illumination or Brightness

The contrast of an image can be defined as the relationship between the different intensity values present in the whole image [2]. The contrast is related to how the intensity values are distributed [3]. Suppose they are concentrated toward lower intensity values. In that case, the image will appear darker. In contrast, if the intensity values are concentrated toward higher intensity values, the image will appear bright or illuminated. To exemplify these conditions, we can present examples of increasing the contrast of an image by 50%, which would be equivalent to applying a homogeneous function that multiplies the pixel by 1.5. Another example can be to increase the illumination or brightness by 100 levels, which would be equivalent to employing a function that adds 100 units to the pixel in question. Thus, the homogeneous function can be defined as follows:

$$f_c(I(x,y)) = I(x,y) \cdot 1.5 \qquad (1.3)$$

$$f_h(I(x,y)) = I(x,y) + 100 \qquad (1.4)$$

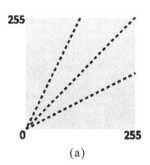 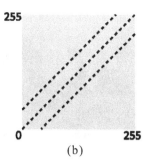

(a)   (b)

FIGURE 1.2
Graphical representation of the mapping generated for the resulting pixel $I'(x, y)$: (a) when changing the value of c in Equation 1.5 with $b = 0$, and (b) when changing the value of b in Equation 1.5 with $c = 1$.

The generic operator $f(\cdot)$, which is used to modify the contrast or illumination in an image, can be formulated as follows:

$$I(x,y) = f(x,y) = c \cdot I(x,y) + b;$$ (1.5)

where c modifies the contrast value and b changes the brightness or illumination value, Figure 1.2 shows graphically the different effects produced by distinct values of c and b.

Figure 1.3 shows the result of applying the above homogeneous operations on an image.

1.2.2 Delimitation of Results by Pixel Operations

When homogeneous operations are used, the calculated pixel value may exceed the limited value defined by the 8-bit grayscale images. Therefore, new pixel values could fall outside the range of 0–255. If this situation happens, the image data type automatically changes from integer (uint8) to float (double). If you write programs in a language such as C, you need to avoid this problem by using appropriate instructions. One example to protect the program when the pixel value exceeds the upper limit is considered as follows:

```
If (Ixy>255)
Ixy=255;
```

The previous operation will have the effect of eliminating any excess produced by the application of the homogeneous operation on the image. This effect is often referred to in the literature as "clamping." Another problem in the use of homogeneous operations performed on pixels occurs when the

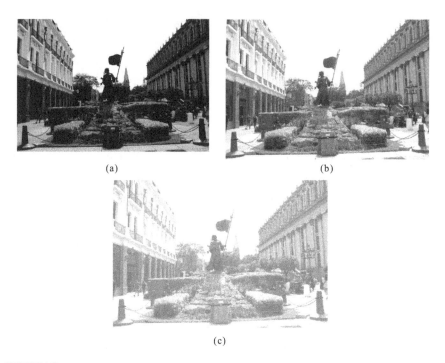

(a)   (b)

(c)

FIGURE 1.3
Examples of applying homogeneous pixel operations. (a) Original image, (b) image with 50% contrast increment, and (c) image with illumination decreased by 100 levels.

calculated value of the new pixel is less than the lower limit defined for an 8-bit grayscale image. This can happen when the value of the illumination is reduced to some levels, producing negative values. This problem, as well as the previous one, is avoided if the program is protected with the following instructions:

```
If (Ixy<0)
Ixy=0;
```

1.2.3 Image Complement

Image complement or inversion is considered a pixel operation in which the pixel value is altered in the opposite direction (by multiplying the pixel value by –1), while on the other hand, a constant intensity value is added. Under this operation, the result falls within the allowed range of values. For one pixel $p = I(x, y)$ on range of values $[0, p_{max}]$ the complement or inversion operation is defined as:

$$f_{inv}(p) = p_{max} - p \tag{1.6}$$

(a)   (b)

FIGURE 1.4
Result of applying the complement pixel operation to an image. (a) Original grayscale image and (b) complement.

To implement the complement operation of an image in MATLAB®, it is necessary to perform the code shown below:

```
I=imread('extension');
 Ig=rgb2gray(I);
IC=255-Ig;
```

Where IC is the result of the complement corresponding to the image stored in I. Figure 1.4 shows the effect of having applied the complement on an image using the previous code in MATLAB.

1.2.4 Segmentation by Threshold

Segmentation by thresholding can be considered a special form of quantification in which the image pixels are divided into two classes depending on their relationship with a predefined threshold value p_{th}. All pixels in the image assume two different values p_0 or p_1 depending on their relationship to the threshold, formally defined as:

$$f_{th}(p) = \begin{cases} p_0 & \text{si } p < p_{th} \\ p_1 & \text{si } p \geq p_{th} \end{cases} \tag{1.7}$$

where $0 < p_{th} < p_{max}$. A frequent application of this operation is the binarization of a grayscale image by considering a $p_0 = 0$ y $p_1 = 1$. An example of applying segmentation by using thresholding on an image is shown in Figure 1.5. The effect of binarization can be clearly seen in the resulting histogram of the image, where the whole distribution is divided into only two parts p_0 y p_1 as shown in Figure 1.6.

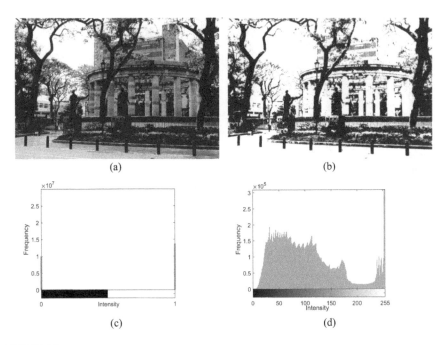

FIGURE 1.5
Example showing the application of segmentation by using thresholding on an image, considering $p_0 = 0$, $p_1 = 1$ y $p_{th} = 80$. In addition, (c) and (d) show the respective histograms of (a) and (b).

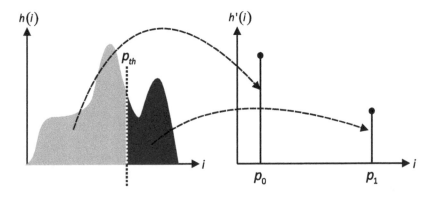

FIGURE 1.6
The effect of the binarization operation on the histogram. The threshold value is p_{th}. (left) Original histogram and (right) histogram resulting from the operation, concentrating their values at two different points. p_0 y p_1.

1.3 Histogram and Pixel Operations

In some cases, the effects of pixel operations can be easily detected through the histogram. Histograms can be considered as a statistical index of the image. It is usually used as an element to assist in the evaluation of important properties of an image [4]. Especially, errors produced in image acquisition are easily recognized through the use of histograms. In addition to the ability to deal with the problems mentioned above, it is also possible to pre-process the image based on the histogram to improve it or to highlight features of the image that will be extracted or analyzed in later processing steps (e.g., by considering a pattern recognition system in the image).

1.3.1 Histogram

Histograms are elements that describe the frequency at which the intensity values (pixels) of the image are distributed. In the simplest case, histograms are best understood when they describe the distribution of grayscale images. An example is shown in Figure 1.7. For a grayscale image $I(u,v)$ with intensities in the range $[0, K-1]$ generate a histogram H with exactly K different values. Therefore, for a typical 8-bit grayscale image, a histogram will use $H = 2^8 = 256$. Each element of the histogram is defined as $h(i)$, corresponding to the number of pixels in the image with an intensity value i, for all values of $0 \leq i < K$. This can be expressed as follows:

$$h(i) = \text{card}^1 \left\{ (u,v) | I(u,v) = i \right\} \tag{1.8}$$

$h(0)$ is then the number of pixels with the value 0, $h(1)$ the number of pixels that have the value of 1, and so on, while finally $h(255)$ represents the number of white pixels (with the maximum intensity value) in the image.

(a)

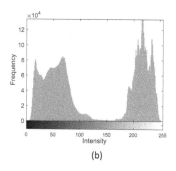

(b)

FIGURE 1.7
(a) 8-bit intensity (grayscale) image and (b) its histogram.

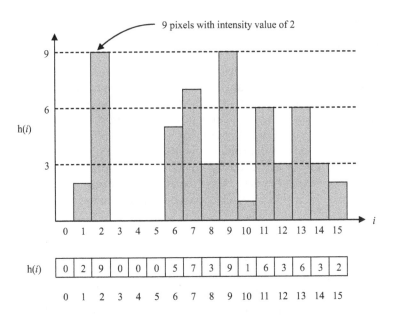

FIGURE 1.8
The vector of a histogram with 16 possible intensity values. The index of the elements of the vector $i = 0...15$ represents the intensity value. The value of 9 of intensity 2 means that in the corresponding image, the intensity value 2 appears 9 times.

As a result of the histogram calculation, a one-dimensional vector h with a length K is obtained, as shown in Figure 1.8 where $K = 16$.

The histogram shows important characteristics of an image, such as its contrast and dynamic range, which are attributed to the image acquisition and need to be evaluated for correcting levels so that image properties can be analyzed more clearly in the post-processing stages.

Evidently, the histogram does not provide information about the spatial distribution of the pixels. Therefore, the information provided by the histogram presents a loss of information about the spatial relationship that the pixels had in the image. Under such conditions, it is impossible to reconstruct an image using only the information from its histogram. To exemplify this fact, Figure 1.9 shows three different images that produce the same histogram.

1.3.2 Image Acquisition Characteristics

Histograms show important characteristics of an image, such as contrast and dynamics, which are problems that occur during image acquisition and have consequences for the subsequent processing steps. In the following, important concepts to consider regarding the acquisition of an image and its histogram are explained.

 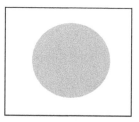 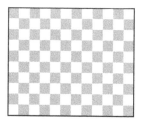

FIGURE 1.9
Three different images that produce the same histogram.

1.3.2.1 Lighting

Illumination errors are recognized in the histogram because there are no pixels in the final or initial region of the intensity scale, while the middle regions of the histogram present a concentration of pixels with different intensity values. Figure 1.10 shows an example of images with different types of illumination. It is possible to observe that the pixels in image (a) cover the entire dynamic (0–255) width of the histogram (b). On the other hand, images (c) and (e) have histograms with intensity values concentrated in whiter colors (values close to 255) and in the darker colors (values close to 0), histograms (d) and (f), respectively.

1.3.2.2 Contrast

The definition of contrast is understood as the range of intensity values that are used in a given image, or, in short, the difference between the maximum and minimum intensity values of the pixels present in the image. A full contrast image uses the full range of intensity levels defined for the image from 0 to $K-1$ (black to white). It is, therefore, easy to observe the contrast of an image using a histogram. Figure 1.11 shows different contrast settings in images from the histograms produced.

1.3.2.3 Dynamics

Under the term dynamics, we understand the number of different pixels that are used in the image. The ideal case in an image is presented when the full range of available intensity values K is used for the image in question. In this case, the whole region of intensity values is covered completely. An image that covers a region of intensity values smaller than the full one $(a_{min} = 0, a_{max} = K-1)$ so that:

$$a_{min} > 0 \text{ or } a_{max} < K-1 \tag{1.9}$$

It produces an image with poor dynamic. It is considered poor since an appropriated dynamic reaches its maximum when all intensity values in that range are present in the image (Figure 1.12).

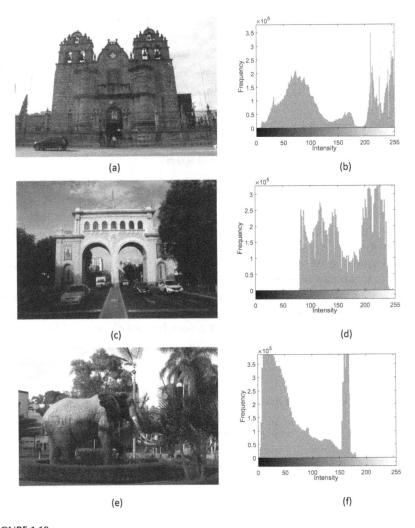

FIGURE 1.10
The figures show how lighting errors are easily detected by the histogram. (a) Image with correct illumination, (c) with high illumination, and (e) with poor illumination. (b), (d), and (f) are the histograms of (a), (c), and (e), respectively.

While the contrast of an image can be high as long as the maximum value of the pixel intensity range is not exceeded, the dynamics of an image cannot be high (except by interpolation of the pixel intensity values). High dynamics represent an advantage for an image because the risk of losing image quality through the following processing steps is reduced. For this reason, digital cameras and professional scanners have a resolution higher than 8 bits, usually 12–14 bits, even if the image display elements have a normal resolution of 256.

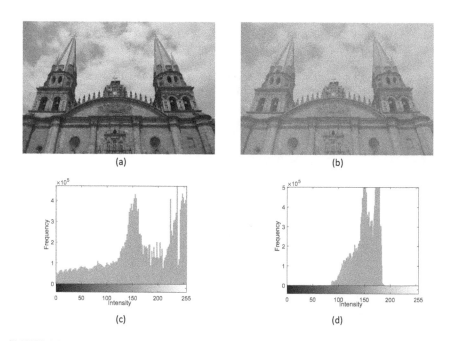

FIGURE 1.11
The figures show different contrasts in images and their respective effects on the histogram.
(a) Normal contrast and its histogram (c); and (b) low contrast and its histogram (d).

1.3.3 Calculating the Histogram of an Image with MATLAB

This section explains MATLAB functions that can be used to calculate and display the histogram of an image contained in the Image Processing Toolbox [5].

1.3.3.1 MATLAB Command Line Function

The function of the image processing toolbox for calculating the histogram of an image has the following format:

```
[counts,x]=imhist(I, n)
```

This function calculates and displays the histogram of the I image. The number of histogram values if n is not specified depends on the type of image involved. If I corresponds to a grayscale image, the function will use 256 values for the calculation and display. If I represents a binary image, the function will calculate the histogram with only two values.

If n is specified, the histogram is calculated and displayed using n intensity values instead of those specified by the image type. The variable counts symbolizes a vector that contains the number of pixels.

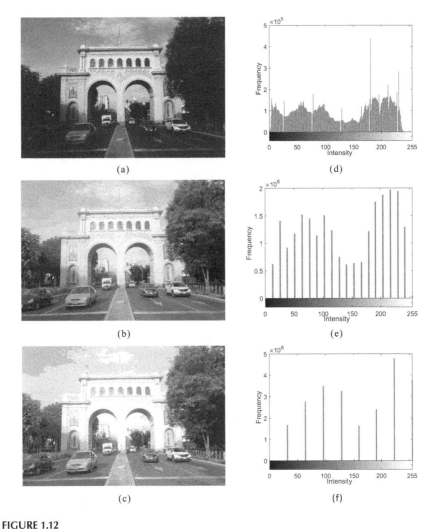

FIGURE 1.12
Different dynamics in an image and their effects on the histogram. (a) High dynamics, (b) low dynamics with 20 intensity levels, (c) very low dynamics with only 8 intensity levels, (d) histogram of (a), (e) histogram of (b), and (f) histogram of (c).

1.3.4 Color Image Histograms

Histograms of color images refer to brightness histograms. They are obtained over the planes from the color image, considering each plane as if it were an independent grayscale image.

1.3.4.1 Brightness Histograms

The brightness histogram of an image is nothing more than the histogram of the corresponding grayscale version of the color image. Since the grayscale

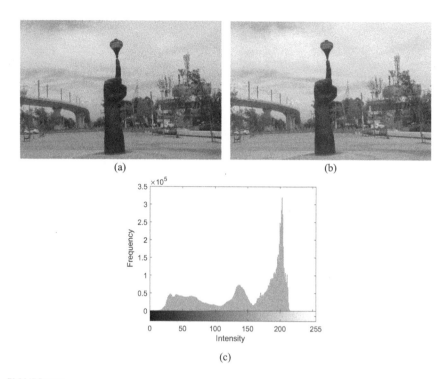

(a)   (b)

(c)

FIGURE 1.13
Brightness histogram of a single plane from a color image. (a) Color image, (b) its grayscale version (luminance image), and (c) the corresponding histogram of (b).

images are extracted from the color image, they represent the histograms of the different planes that compose it. Figure 1.13 shows the luminosity histogram of a color image.

1.3.4.2 Color Component Histograms

Although the luminance histogram considers all color components, it is possible that errors may not be detected in the image. The luminance histogram may appear adequate, even though some color planes are inconsistent.

The histograms of each channel also give additional information on the color distribution in the image. For example, the blue channel (B) usually has a small contribution to the total luminance of the color image. To calculate the color component histograms, each color channel is considered an independent grayscale image from which each histogram is generated. Figure 1.14 shows the luminance histogram h_{LUM} and the histograms of each of the different color planes h_R, h_G y h_B for a typical RGB image.

1.3.5 Effects of Pixel Operations on Histograms

An increase in the illumination (to add a positive constant to all pixel values) of an image causes its histogram to be shifted to the right side so that

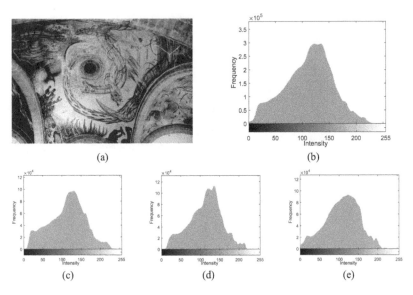

FIGURE 1.14

Histograms of the components from a color image. (a) Original RGB image, (b) histogram of Luminosity (h_{LUM}), (c) histogram of the red channel (h_R), (d) histogram of the green channel (h_G), and (e) histogram of the blue channel (h_B),

the values will tend to approach the upper limit of the allowed dynamic range (to intensity values of 255). On the other hand, an increase in the contrast of some images causes the respective histogram to extend its values within the interval of intensities (0–255). The complement operation on an image or inversion provokes the histogram to reflect itself, but in the opposite direction from its original position. Although the above cases seem straightforward (even trivial), it might be useful to discuss in detail the relationships between pixel operations and the histograms resulting from such operations.

Figure 1.15 illustrates the way in which each region of the image with a homogeneous intensity i belongs to element i in the histogram. This element i corresponds to all pixels having an intensity value of i.

As a result of an operation such as those mentioned above, the histogram value can shift, with the effect that all pixels belonging to this intensity value change. However, what happens when two different intensity values coincide as a result of an operation? In that case, both sets of pixels are merged, and the full amount of both is added together to generate a single intensity value for the histogram. Once different intensity levels have been merged into one, it is not possible to differentiate the subsets of pixels. Consequently, it is not possible to divide them. From the above, it is possible to conclude

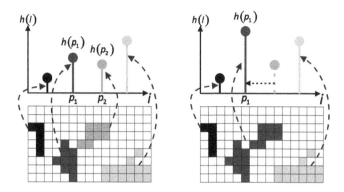

FIGURE 1.15
Histogram values corresponding to a different set of pixels in the image. If a histogram element is shifted as a consequence of an operation, then all pixels of the corresponding set will also be modified in the same way. When two histogram elements $h(p_1)$ y $h(p_2)$ are joined together, their corresponding sets of pixels are also added together and are now non-separable.

that this process or operation is associated with a loss in the dynamics and information of the image.

1.3.6 Automatic Contrast Adjustment

The objective of the automatic adaptation of the contrast is that the pixel values of an image are automatically modified in order to completely cover the allowed range of intensity values. To achieve this, a procedure is performed in which it is considered that the darkest pixel in the image is forced to take the smallest allowable value in the range of intensity values and the brightest pixel to the highest allowable value, while the rest of the pixels between these two values are linearly interpolated within this range [6].

Considering that p_{low} y p_{high} are the current intensity values corresponding to the smallest and highest pixels of an image I, which has a set of intensity values defined by the Interval $[p_{min}, p_{max}]$. To cover the full scale of intensity values of the image, the pixel with the lowest intensity contained in the image

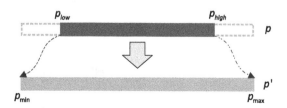

FIGURE 1.16
The auto-contrast operation, in which from Equation 1.10, the pixel value p is linearly interpolated from the interval $[p_{low}, p_{high}]$ to the interval $[p_{min}, p_{max}]$.

is considered as the smallest of the allowable range (zero for an 8-bit grayscale image), and then the contrast (see Figure 1.16) is modified by the factor:

$$\frac{p_{max} - p_{min}}{p_{high} - p_{low}} \tag{1.10}$$

Therefore, the simplest function of contrast adaptation f_{ac} is defined as follows:

$$f_{ac} = \left(p - p_{low}\right)\left(\frac{p_{max} - p_{min}}{p_{high} - p_{low}}\right) + p_{min} \tag{1.11}$$

For an 8-bit grayscale image, the function can be simplified to:

$$f_{ac} = \left(p - p_{low}\right) \cdot \left(\frac{255}{p_{high} - p_{low}}\right) + p_{min} \tag{1.12}$$

The value of the interval $\left[p_{min}, p_{max}\right]$ does not always mean that it is the maximum permissible range of image representation, but it can also represent any range of interest for an image representation. Under such conditions,

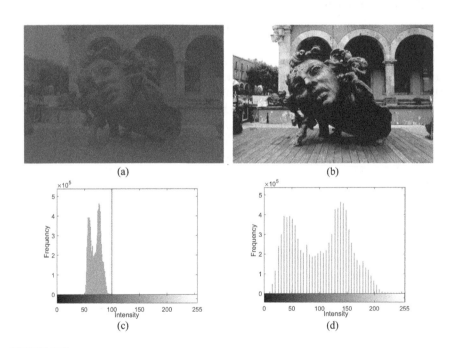

FIGURE 1.17
The effect of the auto contrast operation. (a) Original image with low contrast, (b) enhanced image, (c) histogram of the original image, and (d) histogram of the enhanced image.

this method originally planned to increase the contrast can also be used to represent the image within a particular permissible range p_{low} and p_{high}. Figure 1.17 shows the effect of the auto-contrast operation p'.

As can be seen from Figure 1.17, the self-adjustment of contrast performed by using Equation. 1.11 can produce that the extreme pixel values contained in the image change radically or very little the complete distribution of the resulting histogram. This is because the values of p_{low} and p_{high} from the original histogram involve a very small number of pixels that do not significantly represent the complete distribution. To avoid this problem, some fixed percentages $\left(s_{low}, s_{high}\right)$ are defined from which the distribution is considered significant for both the starting point (dark pixels) and the end element (light pixels) of the distribution. With these percentages, we calculate the new

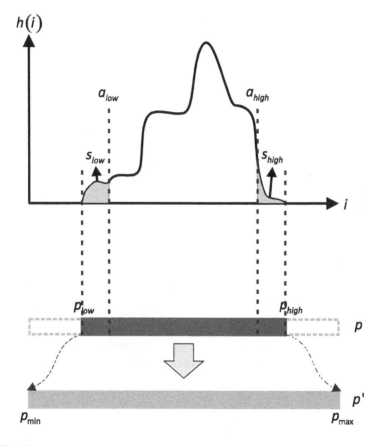

FIGURE 1.18
Auto-contrast operation considers percentage values to generate new boundaries. They now represent the significant values of the distribution. All values between 0 y a_{low} as well as a_{high} and 255 are ignored in the adjustment so that the resulting image reflects an improvement in contrast.

boundaries of the distribution. For this purpose, the lower boundary a_{low} is considered the intensity value at which the number of pixels of lower intensities added together is greater than or equal to s_{low}. Likewise, a_{high} is the upper boundary intensity value at which the number of pixels of higher intensities added together is less than or equal to s_{high}. See Figure 1.18 for an illustration of the process. The values a_{low} y a_{high} depend on the image content and can be easily calculated from the cumulative histogram. $H(i)$ of image I, such that:

$$a_{low} = \min\left\{i\middle|H(i) \geq M \cdot N \cdot s_{low}\right\} \tag{1.13}$$

$$a_{high} = \max\left\{i\middle|H(i) \leq M \cdot N \cdot \left(1 - s_{high}\right)\right\} \tag{1.14}$$

where $M \cdot N$ is the number of pixels in the image I. All values outside the interval a_{low} y a_{high} are not considered for contrast enhancement, while values within this range are linearly scaled to occupy the permissible range $[p_{min}, p_{max}]$. The pixel operation used to perform the auto-contrast operation can be formulated as follows:

$$f_{mac} = \begin{cases} p & \text{si}_{low} & \text{min} \\ (p - a_{low}) & \text{si } a_{low} < p & < a_{high} \\ p & \text{si}_{high} & \text{max} \end{cases} \tag{1.15}$$

In practice, s_{low} y s_{high} are assigned the same value. They typically assume values within the interval [0.5, 1.5]. An example of this operation is provided by the popular image-processing program Photoshop, where the value of s is set to $s_{low} = 0.5$ in order to perform auto-adjustment of the contrast in images.

1.3.7 Cumulative Histogram

The cumulative histogram is a variant of the normal histogram. It provides important information for performing pixel-by-pixel operations on images (point operations), for example, to balance a histogram. The cumulative histogram $H(i)$ is defined as:

$$H(i) = \sum_{j=0}^{i} h(j) \quad \text{para } 0 \leq i < K \tag{1.16}$$

The value of $H(i)$ is then the sum of all the elements below the specified value i of the "classical" histogram $h(j)$ with the values $j = 0 \ldots i$. or the value obtained considering the immediately preceding value

$$H(i) = \begin{cases} h(0) & \text{para } i = 0 \\ H(i-1) + h(i) & \text{para } 0 \leq i < K \end{cases} \tag{1.17}$$

The cumulative histogram is, according to its definition, a monotonically increasing function with a maximum value of

$$H(K-1) = \sum_{j=0}^{K-1} h(j) = MN \tag{1.18}$$

Figure 1.19 shows an example of the cumulative histogram.

1.3.8 Histogram Linear Equalization

A frequent problem is the adaptation of different images to the same distribution h_{eq} of intensity levels, either to improve their print quality or to be able to compare them properly. Balancing a histogram means, by using a pixel operation, changing the image in such a way that it shows a histogram, as far

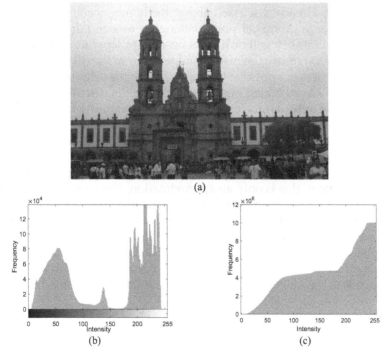

FIGURE 1.19
(a) Original image, (b) histogram of (a), and (c) the cumulative histogram of (a).

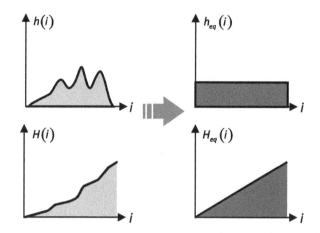

FIGURE 1.20
Representation of the equalization process of a histogram. Using a pixel operation on an image with the original histogram $h(i)$, the idea is to obtain the histogram $h_{eq}(i)$, the cumulative histogram $H(i)$ and the balanced version represented by $H_{eq}(i)$ as the effect of the operation.

as possible, distributed over all intensity levels (see Figure 1.20). Since we are dealing with discrete distributions, this is only possible at the approximation level because, as already discussed above, the homogeneous operations can only shift or merge groups of pixels belonging to a certain intensity level. However, once they are together, it is not possible to separate them. Therefore, it is not possible to remove the histogram peaks from the distribution. Under such conditions, it is not possible to produce, from the original histogram, an ideal histogram h_{eq}, where all gray levels are equally distributed. Instead of this, it is possible only to transform the image so that the histogram shows an approximation to the balanced distribution of gray levels. Such an approximation can be achieved by the cumulative histogram $H(i)$. An important feature of this transformation is that a version of the cumulative histogram H_{eq} represents a balanced (target) distribution. Obviously, as presented in the previous statement, this is only an approximation. However, it is possible in this way to use a pixel operation that shifts the histogram elements in such a way that the cumulative histogram of the image shows at least approximately an increasing linear function, as exemplified in Figure 1.20.

The pixel operation $f_{eq}(p)$ required to balance the histogram of an image is calculated from its cumulative histogram. For an image with a resolution $M \times N$ pixels in the range of $[0...K-1]$ the operation can be defined as follows:

$$f_{eq}(p) = \left[H(p) \cdot \frac{K-1}{MN} \right] \qquad (1.19)$$

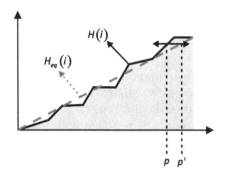

FIGURE 1.21
Through the use of the correct pixel operation f_{eq} the intensity value p is shifted to p' in such a way that it best approximates the cumulative target histogram $H_{eq}(i)$.

The function defined in Equation 1.13 presents a monotonical behavior because this function corresponds to the cumulative histogram experiments, a behavior in which it is constantly incremented. $H(p)$ and the other parameters K, M, and N are only constants. An image whose histogram is already well distributed over all its intensity levels would not represent any change when applying the pixel operation that balances the histogram. Figure 1.21 shows the result on an image after having equalized its histogram linearly. It can be noted that for inactive pixels (those intensity values that do not exist in the original image), when they are considered in the cumulative histogram, the graph presents the same value as its previous neighbor value. For example, consider that there are no pixels in the original image of intensity level 10. Their value in the histogram will be $h(10) = 0$, but their value in the cumulative histogram will be $H(10) = H(9)$. This, although it would seem to be a negative consequence of the pixel operation used to balance the histogram (Equation 1.11). As a consequence, intensity values that do not exist in the original image will not finally appear in the balanced image.

$$faD(i) = \frac{H(i)}{H(K-1)} = \frac{H(i)}{\text{Sum}(h)} = \sum_{j=0}^{i} \frac{h(j)}{\text{Sum}(h)} = \sum_{j=0}^{i} hN(i)$$

$$0 \leq i < K \qquad\qquad (1.20)$$

The function $faD(i)$ is, like the cumulative histogram, monotonically increasing, so it follows that:

$$faD(0) = hN(0) \qquad\qquad (1.21)$$

$$fdD(K-1) = \sum_{i=0}^{K-1} hN(i) = 1 \tag{1.22}$$

Through this statistical formulation, it is possible to model the image as a random process. The process is usually considered to be homogeneous (i.e., independent of the position in the image). Thus, each pixel in the image $I(x,y)$ is the result of a random experiment with a random variable i.

1.4 Gamma Correction

So far, in this book, the word "intensity" has been used several times, with the understanding that the pixel values of an image are somehow related to these concepts. However, how does the value of a pixel actually relate to the amount of light on a monitor or to the number of toner particles that the laser printer needs to form a certain intensity value on the paper? In general, the relationship between the intensity value of a pixel and its respective physical measurements is complex and, in all cases, non-linear. Therefore, it is important to know at least approximately the nature of these relationships and thus to be able to predict the appearance of images on different media.

Gamma correction is a pixel operation that compensates for the different image acquisition conditions and allows the display of different characteristics by using a general space of intensities [7]. The expression gamma originally comes from classical photography, where there is an approximately logarithmic relationship between the amount of illumination and

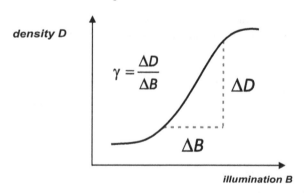

FIGURE 1.22
Illumination function for photography. The function relates the logarithmic magnitude of the illumination to the resulting photographic film density over a relatively large region. The slope of the function is defined as gamma (γ) of the photographic film $\gamma = \dfrac{\Delta D}{\Delta B}$.

the resulting density of the photographic film. The so-called illumination function represents this relationship and is distributed over a relatively large region in the form of an ascending line (see Figure 1.22). The slope of the illumination function within its dispersion region is traditionally defined as the gamma of the photographic film. Later in the television industry, the problem of image distortion due to the nonlinearity of the cathode ray tube was confronted, and the concept of gamma was adopted to describe it. Therefore, the television signal is corrected by the television station before sending it to the receiver, which is called gamma correction, so this correction compensates for the distortion made by the TV.

1.4.1 The Gamma Function

The basis for the gamma correction is the gamma function, which can be defined as follows:

$$b = f_\gamma(a) = a^\gamma$$

$$b = f_\gamma(a) = a^\gamma$$

$$a \in \mathbb{R}, \gamma > 0$$

(1.23)

where the parameter γ is the so-called gamma factor. The gamma function is used only within the interval $[0,1]$, and the function produces a value from $(0,0)$ to $(1,1)$. As shown in Figure 1.23, when $\gamma = 1$, we have $f_\gamma(a) = a$ (identity), generating a line from $(0,0)$ to $(1,1)$. For values of $\gamma < 1$, the function is displayed above the line. For the case $\gamma = 1$, if $\gamma > 1$, the function is below the line, where the curvature of the function increases in both directions (above and below the line) as long as γ is different from 1.

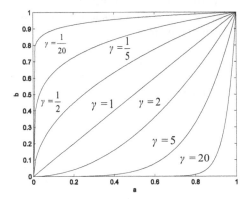

FIGURE 1.23
Gamma function $b = a^\gamma$ for different values of γ.

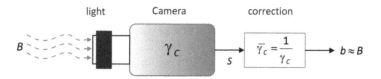

FIGURE 1.24
Principle of gamma correction. To correct the distortion γ_c presented by a camera, it is necessary to apply the gamma correction $\overline{\gamma}_c$ in such a way that the combination of both generates
the elimination of the distortion.

The gamma function is controlled only by the parameter γ and behaves
with monotonical increments in the interval [0,1], so it is invertible, such that:

$$a = f_\gamma^{-1}(b) = b^{1/\gamma} = f_{\overline{\gamma}}(b) \tag{1.24}$$

The same is applicable to the case of the gamma value with $\overline{\gamma} = \dfrac{1}{\gamma}$.

The specific values of γ for different devices are usually specified by the
manufacturer and obtained from measurements. For example, the nominal
values for γ of a standard cathode ray tube are between 1.8 and 2.8, with a
typical value of 2.4 for a standard LCD monitor.

1.4.2 Use of Gamma Correction

To illustrate the use of gamma correction, it is assumed that a camera distorts
the image with a value γ_c. It produces an output signal s because of the occur-
rence of the illumination value under the following relationship:

$$s = B^{\gamma_c} \tag{1.25}$$

To compensate for this distortion, we apply an inverse gamma correction to
the camera output signal. $\overline{\gamma}_c$ will allow us to recover the original signal. This
operation can be formulated as follows:

$$b = f_{\overline{\gamma}_c}(s) = s^{1/\gamma_c} \tag{1.26}$$

From this formulation, it can be observed that:

$$b = s^{1/\gamma_c} = \left(B^{\gamma_c}\right)^{1/\gamma_c} = B^{\frac{\gamma_c}{\gamma_c}} = B^1 = B \tag{1.27}$$

The corrected signal b is identical to the light intensity. Under this operation, the distortion produced by the camera is eliminated. Figure 1.24 shows
an illustration of this process. The rule of thumb is to find the distortion γ_D for
the device in question and compensate for it through gamma correction $\overline{\gamma}_D$.

Everything discussed above assumes that all values are in the interval [0,1]. Obviously, this is not always the case, particularly when dealing with digital images in the range [0,255]. Considering this, for applying the gamma correction, the only thing to do is to scale the image interval to values between 0 and 1 and then apply the gamma correction as discussed in this section.

1.5 MATLAB Pixel Operations

Once we have covered the theoretical foundations in previous sections, we will present how to use MATLAB tools to perform pixel operations on images. These tools involve using MATLAB as a programming language (.m file extension) and functions belonging to the image processing and computer vision toolboxes.

1.5.1 Changing Contrast and Illumination in MATLAB

To increase the contrast using MATLAB, it is necessary to multiply the image by a positive constant so that the histogram of the resulting image becomes wider. The following command assumes that A is an image, and the contrast is raised by 50% so that the image is multiplied by 1.5, leaving its result in B.

```
>>B=A*1.5;
```

To increase the illumination of an image in MATLAB, add to the image the number of levels to which you want to increase the illumination. With this operation, we will make the histogram move in any direction according to the added number of levels. The following command assumes that we want to increase the illumination of image A by 10 levels, so we add 10 to this matrix, producing the result in B.

```
>>B=A+10;
```

1.5.2 Segmenting an Image by Thresholding Using MATLAB

Although segmentation and binary image processing will be covered in depth in another chapter, this section briefly introduces thresholding, but only as a pixel operation, and how to perform it using MATLAB commands.

Using the functions of the MATLAB image processing toolbox, it is possible to segment an image depending on the intensity level of the objects presented in the scene.

To perform the segmentation process by thresholding, it is only necessary to define the intensity level (threshold) from which the elements of the image can be classified into two classes. Those above this value will be considered as a particular class, while those below this value will be considered another class.

1.5.2.1 Command Line Segmentation

The simplest binarization process that can be conducted by MATLAB is logical operations. The way to do this is by using the overloaded property of the logical operations. These operations, in the case of matrices (images), imply the evaluation of the logical condition for each element. The result of this operation produces ones and zeros for those elements that have fulfilled the logical condition. On the other hand, the elements with a value of zero represent those pixels whose evaluation of the condition is false. For example, we would have in the command line:

```
>>B=A>128;
```

The resulting matrix *B* will be composed of ones and zeros. Ones at those positions of *A* where the pixel values are greater than the threshold 128, while zeros at those points of A where the pixels did not meet the condition.

1.5.3 Contrast Adjustment with MATLAB

MATLAB contains the function imadjust, which allows us to adapt the contrast of images to increase, decrease or adjust it. The function prototype presents the following structure:

```
J=imadjust (I)
J=imadjust(I,[low_in; high_in],[low_out; high_out])
```

$J = $ imadjust(I) maps the intensity values of the image I to new intensity values in image J such that from 1% of the data $\left(s_{low} = s_{high} = 1\%\right)$ are considered to define the lower and upper limits of intensities of the image I. From these limits, it will be adjusted the contrast of the resulting image J. As already discussed above, the fact of not considering the limits of image I, but only a percentage, allows us to improve the contrast considering the complete amount of the data. Under such conditions, it is possible to improve the contrast of the image even in those cases where the contrast covers the entire image range but not significantly.

$J = $ imadjust(I,[low_in; high_in],[low_out; high_out]) maps the values of the image I to new values of J, such that the values of image low_in and high_in are mapped to the new values low_out and high_out of image J. The values below low_in and high_in of the image

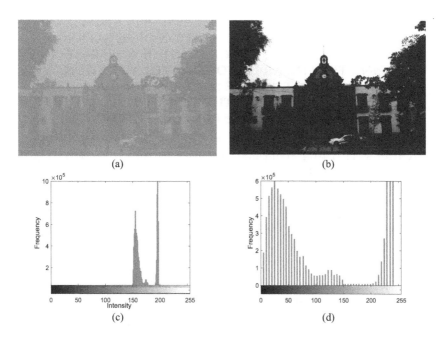

FIGURE 1.25
Result of applying the imadjust function. (a) Original image, (b) image resulting from applying the imadjust function, (c) histogram of the original image, and (d) histogram of the contrast-corrected image.

I are not considered. It is possible to delimit the boundaries with the empty matrix [], which means defining the boundaries with the permissible values for each type of image [0,1].

There are some additional variants of this function that, apart from considering the contrast enhancement, allow us to further scale the contrast by means of a parameter (SP). Through this parameter, it is possible to represent the way in which the images I and J are related when scaled. The structure of the function is as follows:

```
J = imadjust(I,[low_in; high_in],[low_out; high_out], SP)
```

This function transforms the values of I to obtain the values of J, as explained above. However, if SP is less than 1, the mapping is scaled up (brighter) for the J image values, while if SP is greater than 1, the scaling is done down (darker). For the case where SP is one, the adjustment is simply linear. Figure 1.25 shows the effect of applying the imadjust function to an image.

PROGRAM 1.1. IMPLEMENTATION OF EQUATION 1.28 TO ENHANCE THE CONTRAST OF AN IMAGE USING THE LINEAR HISTOGRAM EQUALIZATION TECHNIQUE, WHERE IMG IS THE SOURCE IMAGE AND IMGEQ IS THE IMAGE WITH THE ENHANCED CONTRAST BY EQUALIZATION

```
%%%%%%%%%%%%%%%%%%%%%%%%%%%%%%%%%%%%%%%%%%%%%%%%%%%%%%%%%%%%%%%%
%Program 1.1: Image contrast enhancement using the linear %
%equalization technique                                     %
%%%%%%%%%%%%%%%%%%%%%%%%%%%%%%%%%%%%%%%%%%%%%%%%%%%%%%%%%%%%%%%%
%Erik Cuevas                                       %
%Alma Rodríguez                                     %
%%%%%%%%%%%%%%%%%%%%%%%%%%%%%%%%%%%%%%%%%%%%%%%%%%%%%%%%%%%%%%%%
clear all
close all

img = imread('image.jpg');
% The image is converted to a grayscale image
img = rgb2gray(img);
% The intensity image is displayed.
figure
imshow(img)
% Display the original histogram of the image
figure
imhist(img)
% Display the cumulative histogram
h = imhist(img);
H = cumsum(h);
figure
bar(H)
% Linear equalization
[m,n] = size(img);
for r = 1:m
  for c = 1:n
    ImgEq(r,c)=round(H(img(r,c)+1)*(255/(m*n)));
  end
end
ImgEq = uint8(ImgEq);
% Enhanced image and histogram are shown
figure
imshow(ImgEq)
figure
imhist(ImgEq)
h2 = imhist(ImgEq);
H2 = cumsum(h2);
figure
bar(H2)
```

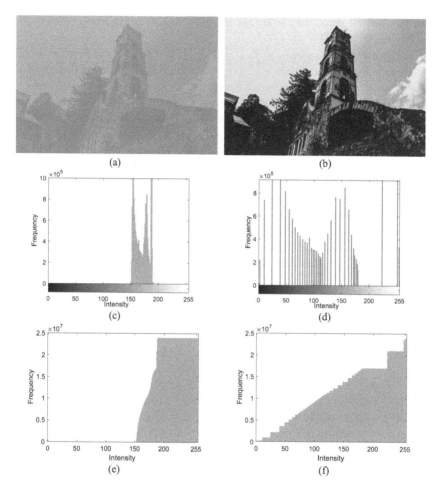

FIGURE 1.26

Result of applying the code described in Program 1.1. (a) Original intensity image, (b) contrast-enhanced image, (c) histogram of the original image, (d) histogram of the enhanced image, (e) cumulative histogram of the original image, and (f) cumulative histogram of the enhanced image.

1.5.4 Histogram Equalization Using MATLAB

The problem of adapting different images to the same distribution of intensity levels, either to improve their print quality or to compare them properly, can be implemented using MATLAB. Equalizing a histogram, as already discussed in previous sections, means modifying it by using a pixel operation of the image in such a way that it shows a histogram with a desired distribution. To solve the equalization problem, the cumulative histogram is used, and among its properties is that it represents an equalized distribution. Obviously, the above statement is only an approximation. However, it is possible to use a pixel operation that shifts the histogram elements so that the cumulative histogram of the image shows at least approximately an increasing linear function.

The required pixel operation $f_{eq}(p)$ to equalize the histogram of an image is calculated from its cumulative histogram, which is defined by Equation 1.28. By implementing this process in a MATLAB program, one could equalize the histogram of an image in a linear way. Program 1.1 shows the implementation of the linear equalization of the histogram of an image.

The results shown in Figure 1.26 were obtained after applying the code described in Program 1.1. From the figure, the result of the contrast improvement can be clearly observed and can be analyzed by reviewing the corresponding histograms.

The MATLAB image processing toolbox implements the histeq function, which allows equalizing the histogram of images to increase their contrast. histeq increases the contrast of an image by transforming the intensity levels of the image so that the histogram of the output image is close to a specific histogram considered as a reference. The function has the following structure:

```
J = histeq(I, hgram)
J = histeq(I, n)
```

J = histeq(I, hgram) transforms the intensity values of the image I so that the cumulative histogram of image J is close to the one considered as reference hgram. The vector hgram must have a length that depends on the type of image and its characteristics. For example, for images of type uint8, we have a length of 256. To perform the transformation of the intensity levels of I, we select a function f_T (pixel operation), which produces a cumulative histogram that minimizes the association defined by:

$$\sum_i \left| H_{f_T}\left(f_T(i)\right) - H_{hgram}(i) \right| \tag{1.28}$$

where H_{f_T} is the cumulative histogram of the image transformed by the function f_T and H_{hgram} the cumulative histogram is considered a reference to which we want to approximate H_{f_T} by choosing f_T.

If the vector hgram is not used in the function histeq, it is considered that the transformation performed on the image I is done so that its histogram approaches a response that is as flat as possible.

J = histeq(I, n) transforms the intensity values of the image I, returning an image with only n different intensity values. The transformation is performed by mapping the intensity levels of image I to n different values of image J so that the histogram of J is approximately flat.

Figure 1.27 shows the result of applying the function histeq to an image. In this example, the vector hgram has not been given as an argument. Therefore, the transformation of the intensity values of the source image is

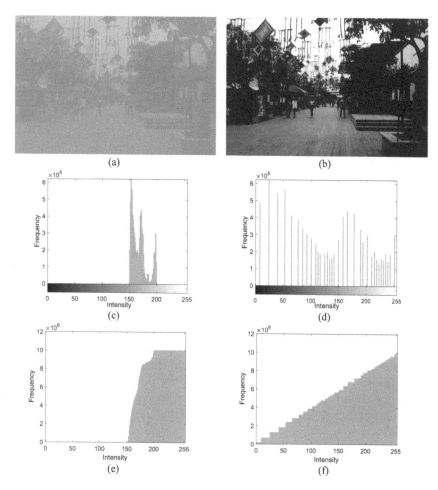

FIGURE 1.27

Result of applying the function `histeq`. (a) Source image, (b) result image, (c) histogram of the source image, (d) flattened histogram resulting from the operation performed by histeq, (e) cumulative histogram of the source image, and (f) cumulative histogram of the resulting image.

performed so that the histogram of the resulting image is approximately flat, which results in a cumulative histogram similar to a straight line.

1.6 Multi-Source Pixel Operations

Sometimes it will be necessary to perform pixel operations where the intensity value of the resulting pixel depends not only on the pixel in question in

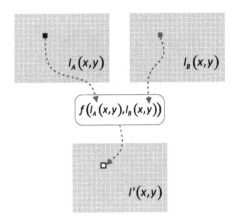

FIGURE 1.28
Representation of pixel operations, in which the resulting pixel depends on the value of pixels from different images, keeping the same position.

an image but also on other pixels in different images. Figure 1.28 shows a representation of such operations.

As can be seen from Figure 1.28, the resulting pixel is obtained from the application of a function that operates on the two pixels from two different images. It is also considered that all the pixels participating in the function are from two different images with the same position. The value from this operation represents the result, which is in the same position as its sources.

1.6.1 Logical and Arithmetic Operations

Logical and arithmetic operations performed between images, such as addition, subtraction, AND, and OR, can be performed pixel by pixel. An important point to consider is the fact that these operations may result in values that are outside the permissible range for the image, so sometimes a change of scale is required.

1.6.1.1 Sum

The sum of the two images I_A and I_B is defined as:

$$I'(x,y) = I_A(x,y) + I_B(x,y) \tag{1.29}$$

A common application of this operation is to superimpose one image on another to achieve a blending effect (see Figure 1.29), as well as to add an image with artifacts or dots in different positions to simulate noise patterns.

(a) (b)

(c)

FIGURE 1.29
Superposition of images by applying the sum operator between two images. (a) Image 1, (b) image 2, (c) superposition of images 1 and 2.

1.6.1.2 Subtract

The difference between the two images I_A and I_B is defined as:

$$I'(x,y) = I_A(x,y) - I_B(x,y) \tag{1.30}$$

This operation is commonly used for image segmentation and enhancement. Another important use of image subtraction is in the case of movement detection [8]. If two images taken at different times are considered, T_1 y T_2, and we obtain their difference. What we will find with it is the change in position of the pixels that were part of the object that changed its position. Figure 1.30 shows an example of position change detection by subtracting two images taken at different time instants.

1.6.1.3 AND and OR

These operations are performed between binary images using the truth table for both logic functions. Therefore, in the case of AND, both pixels must be

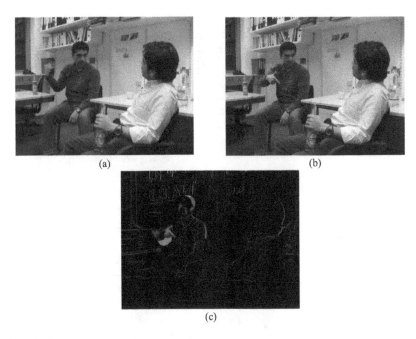

(a)

(b)

(c)

FIGURE 1.30
Movement detection by subtracting images taken at different time instants. (a) Image 1 taken at instant 1, (b) image 2 taken at instant 2, and (c) subtraction of image 1 and 2.

(a)

(b)

(c)

(d)

FIGURE 1.31
Effect of applying the Alpha Blending operation. (a) Image I_B, (b) image I_A, (c) result image I_R with $\alpha = 0.3$, and (d) result image I_R with $\alpha = 0.7$.

one in order to generate a pixel one in the resulting image, while in the case of the OR function with one of the pixels of the image being one is sufficient reason to generate one in the output image. For any other combination in both cases, the pixel will be zero in the output image. These functions have their main activity in block processing, where only those pixels considered in a certain region will be considered in the processing, while the others will be set to zero or simply not taken into account.

1.6.2 Alpha Blending Operation

The alpha blending or compositing operation is used to combine two images, where each pixel of the resulting image is a linear combination of the pixels of the two images considered as sources. That is, if we have two images and we apply the alpha blending operation to combine them, each pixel of the resulting image will be a linear combination of both images, defined by the following equation:

$$I_R(x,y) = (1-\alpha) \cdot I_A(x,y) + \alpha \cdot I_B(x,y) \tag{1.31}$$

By means of this operation, it is possible to blend two images. The background image is represented by the image I_A. The image I_B is considered transparent in the background I_A. The association of these two images is controlled by the transparency factor α, which is defined in the interval [0,1]. Figure 1.31 shows the effect of applying this operation to two images, considering different values of α.

References

[1] Gonzalez, R. C., & Woods, R. E. (2008). *Digital image processing* (3rd ed.). Prentice Hall.

[2] Jain, A. K. (1989). *Fundamentals of digital image processing*. Prentice Hall.

[3] Woods, R. E. (2015). *Digital image processing* (4th ed.). Pearson.

[4] Gonzalez, R. C., & Wintz, P. (1977). *Digital image processing*. Addison-Wesley.

[5] Gonzalez, R. C., Woods, R. E., & Eddins, S. L. (2004). *Digital image processing using MATLAB*. Prentice Hall.

[6] Burger, W., & Burge, M. J. (2016). *Digital image processing: An algorithmic introduction using Java*. Springer.

[7] Szeliski, R. (2010). *Computer vision: algorithms and applications*. Springer.

[8] Milanfar, P. (2013). *A tour of modern image processing: From fundamentals to applications*. CRC Press.

2

Spatial Filtering

2.1 Introduction

The essential characteristic of pixel operations considered in Chapter 1 was that the new pixel value of the calculated element finally depends only and exclusively on the value of the original pixel. The result of this operation is located in the same position. Although it is possible to perform many effects on images using pixel operations, there are conditions under which it is not possible to use them to generate specific effects, as it is in the case of blurring (see Figure 2.1) or detection of image edges.

2.2 What Is a Filter?

In an image, noise is observed where, locally, there is an abrupt change in the level of intensity, whether it increases or decreases significantly. Conversely, there are also regions in the image where the intensity of the image remains constant. The first idea of filtering an image is to eliminate noise pixels, replacing them with the average value of their neighbors [1].

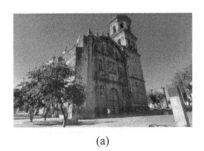

(a)   (b)

FIGURE 2.1
If a pixel operation is used, effects such as blurring or edge detection cannot be performed. (a) Original image and (b) blurred image.

DOI: 10.1201/9781003287414-2

Therefore, to calculate the new value of a pixel $I'(x,y)$, it is used its original value $I(x,y) = p_0$, considering also its eight neighboring pixels $p_1, p_2, \ldots, p_8$ of the original image I. The association among the current pixel p_0 and its neighbors is modeled as the arithmetic average of these nine values:

$$I'(x,y) \leftarrow \frac{p_0 + p_1 + p_2 + p_3 + p_4 + p_5 + p_6 + p_7 + p_8}{9} \tag{2.1}$$

In relative coordinates to the image, the above formulation could be expressed as:

$$I'(x,y) \leftarrow \frac{1}{9} \cdot \begin{bmatrix} I(x-1,y-1) & + & I(x,y-1) & + & I(x+1,y-1) & + \\ I(x-1,y) & + & I(x,y) & + & I(x+1,y) & + \\ I(x-1,y+1) & + & I(x,y+1) & + & I(x+1,y+1) & \end{bmatrix} \tag{2.2}$$

It can also be described in compact form as follows:

$$I'(x,y) \leftarrow \frac{1}{9} \cdot \sum_{j=-1}^{1} \sum_{i=-1}^{1} I(x+i, y+j) \tag{2.3}$$

This formulation shows all the typical elements that describe a filter. This filter is an example of one of the most used types of filters, the so-called linear filters.

Considering the information from Chapter 1, the difference between pixel operations and filters should be clear, especially since the result of filter operations does not only depend on a single pixel of the original image but on a set of them. The current coordinates of the pixel in the original image (x,y) normally define a region $R(x,y)$ of neighbors considered. Figure 2.2 shows the coordinates of the current pixel and its relationship with the considered neighbor region.

The size of the filter region $R(x,y)$ is an important parameter since it determines how many and which neighbors of the original image pixel will be considered to calculate the new pixel. In the example discussed above, a smoothing filter with a region 3×3 was used, which is centered on the coordinate (x,y). With filters of higher sizes, $5 \times 5, 7 \times 7$, or even 31×31 pixels, higher smoothing effects are obtained.

The shape of the filter region can be any. However, the square shape is the most used because, in addition to its ease of calculation (since it is not necessary to calculate the pixel grid by some function, as it would be necessary if it were a circular one), it allows to consider neighboring pixels in all

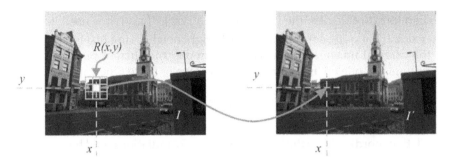

FIGURE 2.2

Principle of filter operations. Each new pixel $I'(x.y)$ is calculated from a certain region $R(x,y)$ of neighbors whose central coordinates are related to the coordinates of the pixel to be calculated.

directions. This is a desirable property of a filter. The relative importance of each neighboring pixel can also be different for a filter. That is, a different weight can be assigned to each pixel in the region depending on its relationship with the central pixel. Therefore, the closest elements to the central pixel are given greater importance, while those located further away are assigned less importance.

There are different alternatives to generating a filter. However, a systematic method is needed to generate a filter that fulfills the requirements of specific uses. There are two different categories of filters: linear and non-linear. The difference between both types of processing is the way in which the pixel within the processing region $R(x,y)$ is connected with the operation, which can be linear or non-linear [2]. In the remainder of the chapter, both types of filters will be discussed, and some practical examples will also be shown. The main operation in filtering corresponds to the sum of the multiplications of each pixel by the coefficients in a neighborhood defined by the matrix. This matrix of coefficients is known in the computer vision community as a filter, mask, kernel, or window.

2.3 Spatial Linear Filters

In linear filters, the intensity values of the pixels within the processing region are combined linearly to generate the resulting pixel [3]. An example of this type is presented in Equation 2.3, where nine pixels that are part of a region 3×3 are linearly combined in a sum multiplied by the factor (1/9). With the same mechanism, a multiple numbers of filters can be defined with different behaviors on an image. To obtain different effects over the image, it is necessary to define the weights of the kernel. These weights are the values that assign the relative importance of each pixel in the linear combination.

2.3.1 The Filter Matrix

Linear filters are fully specified by defining the size and shape of the processing region, as well as the corresponding weights or coefficients that determine how linearly the pixel values of the original image are combined. The values of these coefficients or weights are defined in the filter matrix $H(i, j)$ or simply mask. The size of the matrix $H(i, j)$ determines the size of the filter processing region $R(x, y)$, and its values define the weights in which the corresponding image intensity values are multiplied to obtain their linear combination [4]. Therefore, the filter to smooth an image considered in Equation 2.3 can be defined by the following filter mask:

$$H(i, j) = \begin{bmatrix} 1/9 & 1/9 & 1/9 \\ 1/9 & 1/9 & 1/9 \\ 1/9 & 1/9 & 1/9 \end{bmatrix} = \frac{1}{9} \begin{bmatrix} 1 & 1 & 1 \\ 1 & 1 & 1 \\ 1 & 1 & 1 \end{bmatrix} \qquad (2.4)$$

From Equation 2.4, it can be seen that each of the nine pixels that are defined in the mask contributes to one-ninth of the final value of the resulting pixel.

Fundamentally, the filter matrix $H(i, j)$, like an image, is a two-dimensional discrete real function. Therefore, the mask has its own coordinate system, where the origin is its center. Under such conditions, we will have positive or negative coordinates (see Figure 2.3). It is important to note that the coefficients of the filter matrix outside its defined coordinates are zero.

2.3.2 Filter Operation

The effect of a filter on an image is completely defined by the coefficients of the matrix $H(i, j)$. The way in which the filtering process is carried out on the image is shown in Figure 2.4. This process can be described as follows:

For each pixel (x, y) of the image, the following steps are carried out:

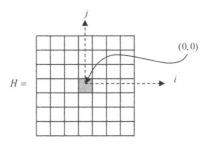

FIGURE 2.3
Mask grid and its corresponding coordinate system.

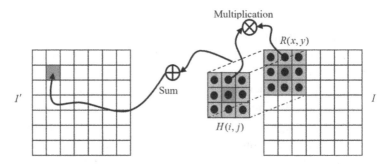

FIGURE 2.4

Linear filters. The origin of the filter coefficient matrix is placed at the original image I pixel (x,y). The filter coefficients $H(i,j)$ are multiplied by the corresponding pixels of the image, thus obtaining nine different products. All products are added, and the result is placed at the position (x,y) of the result image I'.

1. The filter matrix $H(i,j)$ is positioned on the original image I at pixel $I(x,y)$ in such a way that its coordinate center $H(0,0)$ coincides with it.

2. The pixels of the image that are located within the region $R(x,y)$ defined by the filter matrix $H(i,j)$ are multiplied by the corresponding coefficients for each position $I'(x,y)$ of the filter matrix, and the partial result of each of these multiplications is added.

3. The outcome is placed at the position (x,y) of the resulting image.

In other words, all pixels in the resulting image are calculated using the following equation:

$$I'(x,y) = \sum_{(i,j)\epsilon R(x,y)} I(x+i,y+j)\cdot H(i,j) \qquad (2.5)$$

For a typical filter with a matrix of coefficients of size 3×3, the following equation specifies its operation:

$$I'(x,y) = \sum_{j=-1}^{1}\sum_{i=-1}^{1} I(x+i,y+j)\cdot H(i,j) \qquad (2.6)$$

The operation modeled by Equation 2.6 is applied to all coordinates of the image (x,y). Something important that must be considered at this point is that the previous equation is not literally applicable to all the pixels of the image. At the edges of the image, there are elements at which, when centering the matrix of filter coefficients, these do not have correspondence, and a result cannot be clearly established. This problem will be dealt with again with its solutions in Section 2.5.2.

2.4 Calculation of Filter Operations in MATLAB

After knowing how to perform filter operations and being warned to consider their effects on the borders of the image, the way in which it is possible to implement this type of operation through programming in MATLAB® will be shown.

The application of the spatial filters on images is carried out by applying a convolution between the pixel of interest (x,y), its neighbors, and the coefficients of the mask [5]. The spatial filtering processing mechanism is shown in Figure 2.4. The main part of this process lies in the relationship between the coordinates of the filter and those belonging to the image. The process consists of moving the center of the filter from left to right and from top to bottom, performing the corresponding convolution for all pixels in the image. Figure 2.5 shows an illustration of this process. For a filter of size $m \times n$, we have that $m = 2a + 1$ and $n = 2b + 1$, where a and b are non-negative integers. This means that filters are always designed in odd dimensions, with the smallest dimension being 3×3. Although this is not a requirement, working with odd coefficient matrices facilitates the processing as there is a single center, and the operation is done symmetrically.

The value of the new pixel (x,y) generated from the filter depends on the intensity values that correspond to the filter coefficients in a defined region

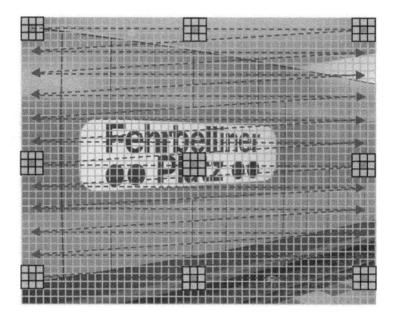

FIGURE 2.5
Application of the spatial filter to an image.

$R(x,y)$. Considering that we have the filter coefficients and the image intensity values shown in Figure 2.6, the new pixel value is computed as follows:

$$I'(x,y) = I(x-1,y-1) \cdot H(-1,-1)$$
$$+I(x-1,y) \cdot H(-1,0) + I(x-1,y+1) \cdot H(-1,1)$$
$$+I(x,y-1) \cdot H(0,-1) + I(x,y) \cdot H(0,0) \qquad (2.7)$$
$$+I(x,y+1) \cdot H(0,1) + I(x+1,y-1) \cdot H(1,-1)$$
$$+I(x+1,y)H(1,0) + I(x+1,y+1)H(1,1)$$

An important aspect of implementation that must be taken into account is the effect that the limits of the image have on the processing. In the limits of the image, several filter coefficients from H will not correspond to some elements from the image I. This problem and how it can be solved will be discussed later. A representation of this problem is shown in Figure 2.7.

A simple solution is to only consider a smaller size of the image in the processing. Under this approach, if we have an image of size $M \times N$ instead of processing the convolution between the image and filter from 1 to N and from 1 to M, the processing will be done by removing the image borders. Therefore, the processing will be conducted from 2 to $N-1$ and from 2 to $M-1$. Applying this, for each filter coefficient, there will be a corresponding pixel of the image.

There are two alternatives to avoid the problem of the lack of correspondence within the limits of the image. The first is to generate a smaller result

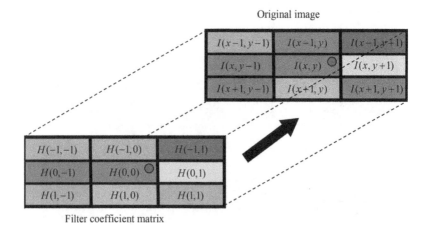

FIGURE 2.6
Spatial filtering process.

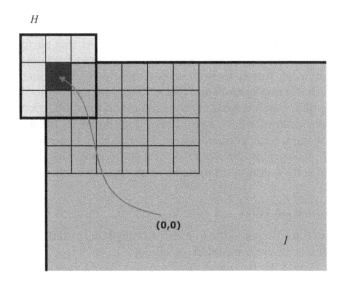

FIGURE 2.7
Problem of the limits of the image in the processing of the convolution. In the pixel (0,0) of the image, if the filter is centered, there will be coefficients of H on which there are no correspondent pixels from the image.

image compared to the original $M - 2 \times N - 1$ (we have previously discussed). Another option is to copy rows and columns from the original image in order to define the missing pixels.

2.5 Types of Linear Filters

The function of a linear filter is specified by the value of its coefficients. Since the coefficients can consist of different values, there are an infinite number of linear filters [6]. From the above, the question is: For what type of effect can a filter be used? And for a certain effect, what are the most suitable filters? In practice, there are two kinds of linear filters: smoothing filters and different filters.

2.5.1 Smoothing Filters

The filters discussed in the preceding sections consider a smoothing effect over the original image. Every linear filter whose coefficient matrix consists only of positive coefficients has in some way a smoothing effect on an image. From this operation, it can be verified that the result is a scaled version of the average value of the region $R(x,y)$ covered by the filter.

2.5.2 The "Box" Filter

The box filter is the simplest and oldest of all the filters that perform smoothing on an image. Figure 2.8 shows (a) the three-dimensional, (b) two-dimensional, and (c) mask functions implemented by this type of filter. Due to the sharp edges that it implements and its frequency behavior, the "Box" filter is a smoothing filter that is not highly recommended for applications. The filter, as can be seen in Figure 2.8a, looks like a box (hence its name) and affects each pixel of the image in the same way (since all its coefficients have the same value). A desirable characteristic of a smoothing filter is that its effect on the image is invariant to rotation. Such a property is called isotropic.

2.5.3 The Gaussian Filter

The Gaussian filter corresponds to a two-dimensional and discrete Gaussian function, which can be formulated as follows:

$$G_\sigma(r) = e^{\frac{r^2}{2\sigma^2}} \text{ or } G_\sigma xy = e^{\frac{x^2+y^2}{2\sigma^2}} \tag{2.8}$$

where the standard deviation σ represents the influence radius of the Gaussian function, as shown in Figure 2.9.

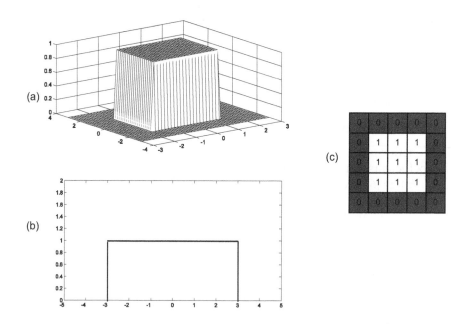

FIGURE 2.8
The Box filter for smoothing. (a) Three-dimensional, (b) two-dimensional, and (c) coefficient matrix that implements the filter.

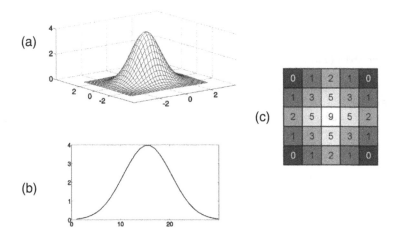

FIGURE 2.9
The Gaussian filter for smoothing. (a) Three-dimensional, (b) two-dimensional, and (c) coefficient matrix that implements the filter.

In the Gaussian filter, the central element of the filter represents the maximum weight that participates in the linear combination of the operation, while the values of the other coefficients have less influence as they move away from the center of the filter.

An important property of this filter is known as isotropy. A problem with the "Box" smoothing filter is that its attenuation also causes a degradation in important characteristics of the image, such as edges (regions of the image where there is a sudden change in intensity) or corners. The Gaussian filter is less harmful in this sense, allowing the smoothing of the regions where the intensity values are homogeneous without diluting the characteristics of the image.

Program 2.1 shows the MATLAB code to implement a filter 3×3 that smooths the image by averaging neighboring pixels, as was discussed in Equation 2.4.

PROGRAM 2.1. IMPLEMENTATION OF THE SMOOTHING 3×3 FILTER IN MATLAB

```
###%%%%%%%%%%%%%%%%%%%%%%%%%%%%%%%%%%%%%%%%%%%%%%%%%%%%%%%%%
% Implementation of the 3x3 filter that smoothes     %
% the image using the average of the neighbors       %
%%%%%%%%%%%%%%%%%%%%%%%%%%%%%%%%%%%%%%%%%%%%%%%%%%%%%%%%%%%%%
% The values of the dimensions of the image are obtained
  Im=imread('Figure 2.1.jpg');
  [m n]=size(Im);
```

```
% The image is converted to double to avoid problems
% in the conversion of the data type
Im=double(Im);
% The original image is copied to the result to avoid
% the image border processing problem.
ImR=Im;
% The filter operation is applied (see Equation 2.4)
% The entire image is traversed with the filter except
% for the border
for r=2:m-1
    for c=2:n-1
        ImR(r,c)= 1/9*(Im(r-1,c-1)+Im(r-1,c)+Im(r-1,c+1)
...

                 +Im(r,c-1)+Im(r,c)+Im(r,c+1)  ...
                  +Im(r+1,c-1)+Im(r+1,c)+Im(r+1,c+1));
    end
end
% The image is converted to an integer to be able to
display it
ImR=uint8(ImR);
```

2.5.4 Difference Filters

If a filter contains negative numbers as part of its coefficients, its operation can be interpreted as the difference between two different sums: The sum of all the linear combinations of the positive coefficients of the filter minus the sum of all the linear combinations due to the negative coefficients within the region defined by the filter $R(x,y)$. If we express this operation mathematically, it can be defined as follows:

$$
I'(x,y) = \sum_{(i,j)\in R^+} I(x+i,y+j)\cdot|H(i,j)|
$$
$$
- \sum_{(i,j)\in R^-} I(x+i,y+j)\cdot|H(i,j)|
$$

(2.9)

where R^+ refers to the part of the filter with positive coefficients $H(i,j) > 0$ and R^- to the part of the filter with negative coefficients $H(i,j) < 0$. As an example, it is shown in Figure 2.10: the Laplace filter of size 5×5. It calculates the difference between the central point (the only positive coefficient with a value of 16) and the negative sum of 12 coefficients with values from –1 to –2. The remaining coefficients are zero and are not considered in the processing. This filter implements the function known as "the Mexican hat," which has the following model:

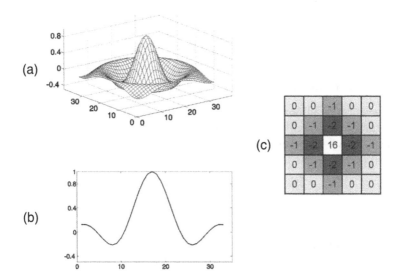

FIGURE 2.10
The Laplace (or Mexican hat) filter. (a) Three-dimensional, (b) two-dimensional, and (c) the coefficients that define the filter.

$$M_\sigma(r) = \frac{1}{\sqrt{2\pi}\sigma^3}\left(1 - \frac{r^2}{\sigma^2}\right)e^{-\frac{r^2}{2\sigma^2}} \tag{2.10}$$

$$M_\sigma(x,y) = \frac{1}{\sqrt{2\pi}\sigma^3}\left(1 - \frac{x^2 + y^2}{\sigma^2}\right)e^{-\frac{x^2+y^2}{2\sigma^2}} \tag{2.11}$$

The models expressed in Equation 2.11 correspond to the same formulation but in one-dimensional and two-dimensional cases. While with filters with positive coefficients, the effect obtained is smoothing, with difference filters (which have positive and negative coefficients), the effect is the opposite. Therefore, the differences between pixel intensity levels are enhanced. For this reason, these types of filters are normally used for edge detection.

2.6 Formal Characteristics of Linear Filters

Until now, the concept of filters has been considered in a simple way so that the reader can get a quick idea of their characteristics and properties. Although this may be sufficient from a practical point of view, there are situations where the understanding of the mathematical properties of their operations allows to design and analyze more complex filters. The operation on which the filters are based is convolution. This operation and its characteristics will be discussed throughout this chapter.

2.6.1 Linear Convolution and Correlation

The operation of a linear filter is based on an operation called linear convolution. This operation allows associating two continuous or discrete functions in one. For two two-dimensional discrete functions I and H the linear convolution is defined as follows:

$$I'(x,y) = \sum_{i=-\infty}^{\infty}\sum_{j=\infty}^{\infty} I(x-i,y-j) \cdot H(i,j) \tag{2.12}$$

Or in compact form:

$$I' = I * H \tag{2.13}$$

The expression in Equation 2.12 is very similar to the one defined in 2.6, with the exception of the limits in the summations for i, j, and the sign in the coordinates $I(x-i, y-j)$. The first difference is explained by the fact that the filter $H(i,j)$ defines a region $R(x,y)$ of influence that contains a finite set of coefficients; outside this region, the coefficients are considered zero or not relevant, so the limit of the sum could be extended without altering the result of the calculation.

Regarding the coordinates, Equation 2.12 can be reformulated again as follows:

$$
\begin{aligned}
I(x,y) &= \sum_{(i,j)\in R} I(x-i,y-j) \cdot H(i,j) \\
&= \sum_{(i,j)\in R} I(x+i,y+j) \cdot H(-i,-j)
\end{aligned}
\tag{2.14}
$$

This expression is again similar to the one defined in Equation 2.5, when the operation of the filter coefficient matrix was defined, only that the coefficient matrix is inverted in the vertical and horizontal directions $H(-i,-j)$. Such an inversion can be interpreted as a 180° rotation of the filter coefficient matrix $H(i,j)$. Figure 2.11 shows how the inversion of the coordinates is modeled by rotating the filter coefficient matrix $H(i,j)$.

A concept very close to convolution is correlation. Correlation is the process of processing the mask or filter $H(i,j)$ through the image (similar to the filter operation defined by Equation 2.5). Therefore, we can say that convolution is equal to correlation only with the difference that the filter coefficient

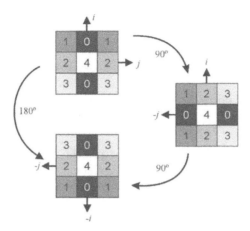

FIGURE 2.11
Coordinate inversion modeling $H(-i,-j)$ by a rotation of 180° of the filter coefficient matrix.

matrix is rotated 180° (with its coordinate axes inverted) before performing the linear combination of coefficients and pixel values. The mathematical operation behind each linear filter operation is convolution, and its result is exclusively dependent on the value of the coefficients of the filter matrix $H(i,j)$. Figure 2.12 shows the convolution process in images.

2.6.2 Linear Convolution Properties

The importance of convolution is due to its very interesting mathematical properties. As will be seen later in this book, there is a close relationship

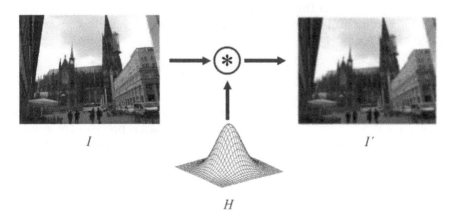

FIGURE 2.12
Convolution with the Gaussian filter. The original image is convolved with the coefficient matrix $H(i,j)$ producing the result.

between convolution, Fourier analysis, and their corresponding methods at frequency [7].

2.6.2.1 Commutativity

The convolution is commutative, which means that:

$$I * H = H * I$$

It represents the same result if the image and the filter exchange order positions in the operation, so there is no difference if the image I with the coefficient matrix $H(i, j)$ is convolved or vice versa. Both functions can exchange positions, obtaining the same result.

2.6.2.2 Linearity

This property implies some important properties. If an image is scaled with a constant a and then this result is convolved by the coefficient matrix H, the same result would be obtained as if the image was first convolved and the result of this operation was scaled by a. That is:

$$(a \cdot I) * H = a \cdot (I * H) \tag{2.15}$$

Furthermore, if two images are added pixel by pixel and then the result is convolved by H, it would give the same result as if both images were firstly convolved and finally the result of each convolved image is added. That is:

$$(I_1 + I_2) * H = (I_1 * H) + (I_2 * H) \tag{2.16}$$

It might be surprising in this context that adding a constant b to an image that is then convolved through the H window of a filter does not produce the same result as if the image was first convolved and then the constant b is added to it. That is:

$$(b + I) * H \neq b + I * H \tag{2.17}$$

The linearity of the filter operations due to the use of convolution is an important theoretical concept; however, in practice, the filter operations are involved in processes that limit this linearity. This fact is provoked by rounding errors or the restriction in the range of images to which they are restricted to visualize them ("Clamping").

2.6.2.3 Associativity

Convolution is an associative operator, which means that the set of operations performed one by one in a sequence could change their grouping order without affecting the original result. That is:

$$A * (B * C) = (A * B) * C \qquad (2.18)$$

The association capacity of the filters is important since the application sequence of a set of filters could be reduced to one, which is normally carried out for the design of coefficient matrices. The opposite case is also valid, where a filter can be broken down into simpler operations performed by smaller filters.

2.6.3 Filter Separability

An immediate consequence of Equation 2.18 is the possibility of describing a filter by the convolution of two or more filters that are tentatively simpler and smaller than the original. Therefore, the convolution performed by a "big" filter on an image could be decomposed by a sequence of convolutions performed by small filters such that:

$$I * H = I * (H_1 * H_2 * H_3 \ldots H_n) \qquad (2.19)$$

The advantage obtained by this separation is to increase the speed of the operations since, although the number of filters is increased, among all of them, being smaller and simpler, they perform fewer operations than the original filter.

2.6.3.1 x-y Separation

Something frequent and important in the use of filters is the separation of a two-dimensional filter H into two one-dimensional filters that operate horizontally H_x and H_y vertically on an image. If we assume that we have two one-dimensional filters H_x and H_y that they operate in each of the directions, then:

$$H_x = \begin{bmatrix} 1 & 1 & 1 & 1 & 1 \end{bmatrix} \text{ or } H_y = \begin{bmatrix} 1 \\ 1 \\ 1 \end{bmatrix} \qquad (2.20)$$

If you want to use both filters, one with the other on image I, both filters can be used as follows:

$$I \leftarrow (I * H_x) * H_y = I * H_x * H_y \qquad (2.21)$$

The same result can be obtained by applying the filter H_{xy} on the image, which is the convolution of both directional filters H_x and H_y, such as follows:

$$H_{xy} = H_x * H_y = \begin{bmatrix} 1 & 1 & 1 & 1 & 1 \\ 1 & 1 & 1 & 1 & 1 \\ 1 & 1 & 1 & 1 & 1 \end{bmatrix} \tag{2.22}$$

Under such conditions, the "Box" H_{xy} smoothing filter can be divided into two one-dimensional filters applied in two different directions on the image. The convolution performed by the full filter H_{xy} needs $3 \times 5 = 15$ operations per pixel in the original image. In the case of the two filters H_x and H_y, they require $3 + 5 = 8$ operations per pixel of the image, which is much less.

2.6.3.2 Gaussian Filter Separation

A two-dimensional filter can be divided into two filters in the $x - y$ directions. Following this methodology, it can be generalized that if you have a function in two dimensions, it is also possible to divide it into two functions, where each function will deal with each dimension in particular. That is, mathematically:

$$H_{x,y}(i, j) = H_x(i) \cdot H_y(j) \tag{2.23}$$

A prominent case is a Gaussian function $G_\sigma(x, y)$ which can be partitioned as the product of two one-dimensional functions as follows:

$$G_\sigma(x, y) = e^{-\frac{x^2 + y^2}{2\sigma^2}} = e^{-\frac{x^2}{2\sigma^2}} \cdot e^{-\frac{y^2}{2\sigma^2}} = g_\sigma(x) \cdot g_\sigma(y) \tag{2.24}$$

Therefore, it is clear that a two-dimensional Gaussian filter $H^{G,\sigma}$ can be divided into a pair of Gaussian $H_x^{G,\sigma}$ and $H_y^{G,\sigma}$ one-dimensional filters. They can be defined as follows:

$$I \leftarrow I * H^{G,\sigma} = I * H_x^{G,\sigma} * H_y^{G,\sigma} \tag{2.25}$$

The Gaussian function decays slowly. Hence, to avoid errors due to rounding of coefficients, it cannot implement values of $\sigma < 2.5$. Therefore, for a filter that incorporates a standard deviation of $\sigma = 10$, a filter of dimensions 51×51 is needed. If the filters were separated in two, as seen above, the filter would implement the operation 50 times faster than using the original filter.

2.6.4 Impulse Response of a Filter

The Delta Dirac δ function is a neutral element in the convolution operation. When this function δ is convolved with an image I, the result is the image I without any change. This effect can be defined as follows:

$$I * \delta = I \qquad (2.26)$$

The Delta Dirac function $\delta(\cdot)$ in the two-dimensional discrete case is defined as:

$$\delta(i, j) = \begin{cases} 1 \text{ for } i = j = 0 \\ 0 \text{ if not} \end{cases} \qquad (2.27)$$

The Delta Dirac function, considered as an image, is visualized as a single bright point at the origin of coordinates around an area of infinite black points. Figure 2.13 shows the Delta Dirac function in two dimensions and how it is conceived as an image.

If the Delta Dirac function is used as a filter and we apply the convolution of this function to an image, the result is again the original image (see Figure 2.14).

The opposite case is also interesting. If the Detla Dirac function is taken as input (as if this were the image) and convolved with a filter, the result would be the matrix of filter coefficients (see Figure 2.15), that is:

$$H * \delta = H \qquad (2.28)$$

The application of this property makes sense if the properties and characteristics of the filter are not known and are desired to be characterized under the condition that the filter to be analyzed is a linear filter. If we apply the impulse function, the filter information can be obtained. The response of a filter to the impulse function is called the impulse response of the filter and is of great value in the analysis and synthesis of engineering systems.

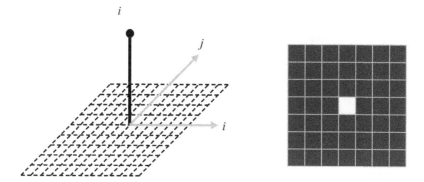

FIGURE 2.13
The Delta Dirac function in two dimensions.

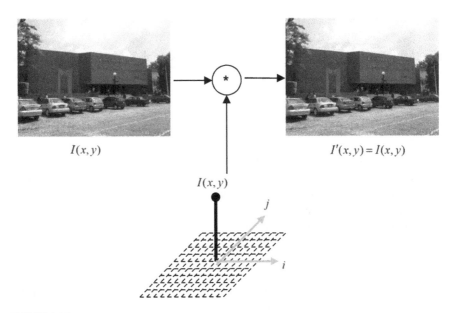

FIGURE 2.14
The result of the Delta Dirac function δ applied to an image I.

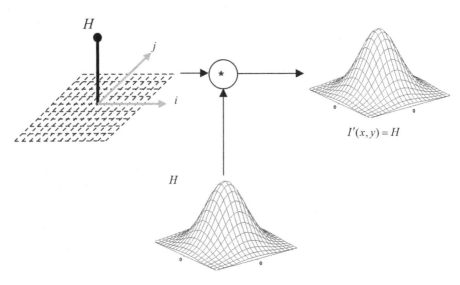

FIGURE 2.15
The result of convolving the function δ and a filter H.

2.7 Add Noise to Images with MATLAB

To test the effectiveness of filters on images, it is necessary to evaluate their effects on images that contain artifacts or structures (noise) that need to be removed. As is logical to suppose, it is difficult to obtain images naturally with these characteristics. That is, it is not easy to obtain these kinds of images from the moment they are taken with a digital camera or scanner [8]. An easier way to get images with these characteristics is simply to artificially produce them, which means taking the image by some means and adding the artifacts through programming code.

Using MATLAB, it is possible, through its programming elements, to induce noise in images. The type of noise that can be modeled and added can be as complex as necessary. In this section, it is shown how to do it in the case of salt and pepper noise. Salt and pepper noise simulates random elements from two categories, white (salt) and black (pepper) pixels, in an image. This type of noise will be used to test the effect of filters designed in the following sections.

Due to the stochastic nature of this type of noise, it will be necessary to use some function in MATLAB that allows randomly giving a value between 1 and the maximum values that describe the size of the image and assigning it to the pair of elements that defines the position (x, y) of the pixel. Once the pixel is chosen, it is assigned a value that can be 255 (in the case of salt) or 0 (in the case of pepper). The MATLAB function that returns a pseudo-random number uniformly distributed between 0 and 1 is rand, whose format can be described as:

```
y = rand
```

where y assumes the value returned by the rand function, the value generated by rand is uniformly distributed between 0 and 1. Therefore, to cover the interval of interest, it is necessary to multiply it by the maximum limit of the interval.

An important aspect is that if the image is only distorted by placing only pixels with values of 0 and 255 when making a visual analysis or simply its display, it becomes somewhat complicated to appreciate the noise pixels. For this reason, it is a better option to add structures. The structure with which you can contaminate the image to generate noise can really be any, although the rectangular one is generally chosen for its simplicity. An important observation is that the structure must, in any case, be smaller than the filter used. Otherwise, the filter will not have the capacity to eliminate distortion. In this case, a structure of 3×2 is chosen since most of the filters proposed to explain their effects on images are of dimension 3×3. Figure 2.16 shows the structure added as noise to the image, considering the relative position of the top left pixel.

(x,y)	$(x+1,y+1)$
$(x+1,y)$	$(x+1,y+1)$
$(x+2,y)$	$(x+2,y+1)$

FIGURE 2.16
Structure added as noise in order to facilitate its visualization instead of the distortion of an individual pixel.

Program 2.2 shows the MATLAB code that allows adding 2000 noise points, where 1000 corresponds to intensity value structures 255 (salt) and 1000 corresponds to intensity value structures 0 (pepper).

PROGRAM 2.2.   MATLAB PROGRAM TO ADD SALT AND PEPPER NOISE TO AN IMAGE

```
###%%%%%%%%%%%%%%%%%%%%%%%%%%%%%%%%%%%%%%%%%%%%%%%%%%%%%%
%%
%                                                      %
% MATLAB script to add salt and pepper noise           %
%                                                      %
%
%%%%%%%%%%%%%%%%%%%%%%%%%%%%%%%%%%%%%%%%%%%%%%%%%%%%%%%%%
%Load image
Ir=imread('fig 2.17.jpg');
Ir = rgb2gray(Ir);
% Make a copy in Ir1 for adding noise
Ir1=Ir;
[row, col]=size(Ir);
% 1000 noise points with value of 255 are calculated
for v=1:1000
    % calculate the positions of each point for x
    x=round(rand*row);
    % for y scales, the value for the maximum interval
    y=round(rand*col);
    % Since MATLAB does not index from 0, the program
    % is protected to start at 1.
    if x==0
        x=1;
    end
    if y==0
        y=1;
    end
    % Borders are recalculated so that the structure % can
    be inserted
    if x>=row
```

```
            x=x-2;
        end
        if y==col
            y=y-1;
        end
        % The structure is inserted with intensity values % of
    255 (salt)
        Ir1(x,y)=255;
        Ir1(x,y+1)=255;
        Ir1(x+1,y)=255;
        Ir1(x+1,y+1)=255;
        Ir1(x+2,y)=255;
        Ir1(x+2,y+1)=255;
        end
    % 1000 noise points with value 0 are calculated
    for v=1:1000
        x=round(rand*row);
        y=round(rand*col);
        if x==0
            x=1;
        end
        if y==0
            y=1;
        end
        if x>=row
            x=x-2;
        end
        if y==col
            y=y-1;
        end
        Ir1(x,y)=0;
        Ir1(x,y+1)=0;
        Ir1(x+1,y)=0;
        Ir1(x+1,y+1)=0;
        Ir1(x+2,y)=0;
        Ir1(x+2,y+1)=0;
    end
    figure
    imshow(Ir)
    figure
    imshow(Ir1)
```

An important consideration is the need to protect the random position where the structure will be placed. If the structure is placed within the limits of the image, it will not be positioned within the image. To avoid this, the program checks if the structure is located in an appropriate position. This process guarantees that the structure will always be located in an appropriate position for its processing. Figure 2.17 shows images that resulted from the execution of Program 2.2.

To save time, you could use the function implemented in the image processing toolbox that allows you to add different types of noise to an image. This section will only explain how to do it for a specific type of salt and pepper noise.

The structure of the function is:

```
g=imnoise(f, 'salt & pepper', 0.2);
```

where f is the image that you want to contaminate with salt and pepper noise and 0.2 is the percentage of pixels (the number of pixels that will be salt and pepper) in the image that you want to contaminate, where 0.2, for example, indicates that 20% of the image pixels will be contaminated. g is the matrix that receives the image contaminated by the configured noise.

(a)   (b)

(c)

FIGURE 2.17
Distortion process of an image with salt and pepper noise carried out using Program 2.2. (a) Original image, (b) added salt and pepper noise (a gray background was placed to appreciate both structures 0 and 255), and (c) the image with the noise.

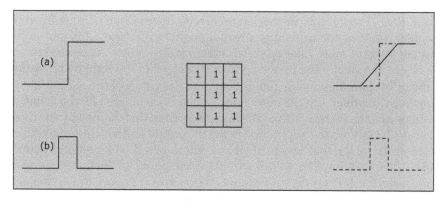

FIGURE 2.18
Linear smoothing degrades important structures in the image, such as edges (a) or lines (b).

2.8 Spatial Non-Linear Filters

The use of linear filters to smooth and remove distortions from images has a great disadvantage; structures present in the image, such as points, edges, and lines, are also degraded (see Figure 2.18). This effect cannot be avoided by using some combination of linear filter coefficients. Therefore, if you want to smooth an image without affecting the quality of the structures present in the image, the use of linear filters is not an alternative [9]. This section presents and explains a special type of filter that allows solving this problem, at least in a better way than linear filters. Non-linear filters are able to eliminate noise without the undesired effects of distortions. Such filters are based on operations whose characteristics and properties are not linear.

2.8.1 Maximum and Minimum Filters

Non-linear filters compute the result at a certain position (x,y) like the previous filters by using a certain region relative to the original image R. The simplest non-linear filters are the maximum and minimum filters. The maximum and minimum filters are correspondingly defined as:

$$I'(x,y) = \min\left\{I(x+i,y+j)|(i,j) \in R\right\}$$
$$= \min\left(R(x,y)\right)$$

(2.29)

$$I'(x,y) = \max\left\{I(x+i,y+j)|(i,j) \in R\right\}$$
$$= \max\left(R(x,y)\right)$$

where $R(x,y)$ represents the region relative to the position (x,y) defined by the filter (most of the time, it is a rectangle of 3×3). Figure 2.19 shows the effect of the minimum filter on different image structures. As can be seen in the figure, the step of the image appears displaced to the right by the action of the minimum filter by an amount equal to the width of the region $R(x,y)$ defined by the filter. On the other hand, a line is eliminated by the action of the filter as long as the width of the line is less than that defined by the filter.

Figure 2.20 shows the application of the minimum and maximum filters on an intensity image that was artificially contaminated with salt and pepper noise. The minimum filter eliminates the white points of the image because, in its operation, it finds the minimum of a region of influence $R(x,y)$ defined by the filter, which, centered on the contaminated white pixel, will replace it with the minimum value found among its neighbors. In the same way, the pixels that have the minimum value allowed by the image (black or pepper) are enlarged in relation to the size A of the filter. The maximum filter naturally presents the opposite effect. That is, pixels representing distortions

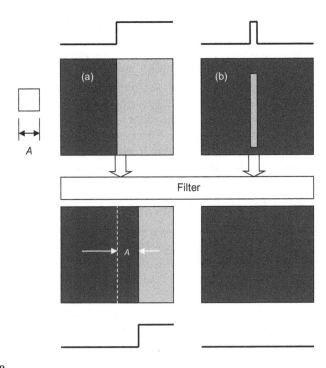

FIGURE 2.19
Effect of the minimum filter on different local shapes in an image. The original image is on top, and the result obtained by operating the filter is on the bottom. The value of A expresses the width of the filter used, which at the same time defines the region R considered by it. The step represented in image (a), due to the effect of applying the filter, is shifted to the right in A units. The line contained in image (b), if its width is less than that of A, disappears due to the effect of the filter operation.

belonging to zero (pepper) or small intensity values will be eliminated, while white structures will also be increased. Figure 2.20 shows the effect of applying the maximum and minimum filters to an image.

2.8.2 The Median Filter

Obviously, it is impossible to build a filter that can remove all the imperfections or noise from the image and, at the same time, keep intact image structures considered important. It is not possible to differentiate which structures are important for the observer and which are not. The median filter is a good compromise in this dilemma.

The effect of fading edges on an image caused by the smoothing effect of linear filters is generally undesirable. The median filter allows you to remove artifacts and unwanted structures in the image without significantly affecting the edges. The median filter belongs to a special class of statistical filters,

(a)

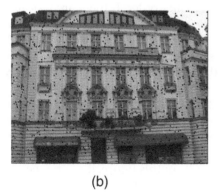

(b)

(c)

FIGURE 2.20
Minimum and maximum filters. (a) The original image to which salt and pepper noise was artificially added (see Section 2.6), (b) image resulting from applying the 3×3 minimum filter, and (c) image resulting from applying the 3×3 maximum filter.

which, in addition to being non-linear, base their actions on some statistical-type operation.

In statistics, the median is the value of a set of data that leaves the same number of elements before and after it. According to this definition, the set of data less than or equal to the median will represent 50% of the data, and those that are greater than the median will represent another 50% of the total from the sample data.

Considering that $x_1, x_2 \cdots, x_n$ is the total set of data ordered in increasing order, the median is defined as follows:

$$M_e = x_{\frac{n+1}{2}} \tag{2.30}$$

If n is odd, M_e will be the central observation of the values once they have been ordered in increasing or decreasing order. If n is even, it will be the arithmetic average of the two central observations, that is:

$$M_e = \frac{x_{\frac{n}{2}} + x_{\frac{n+1}{2}}}{2} \tag{2.31}$$

Therefore, it can be said that the median filter replaces each pixel of the image with the median of the intensity values within the region of influence $R(x,y)$ defined by the filter. This can be expressed as follows:

$$I'(x,y) = M_e\big(R(x,y)\big) \tag{2.32}$$

To calculate the median of the data that integrates the region of interest $R(x,y)$, it is only necessary to execute two steps. First, arrange the intensity values of the image that correspond to the region of influence defined by the filter in vector form. Then, rearrange them in increasing order. If there are repeated values, they will also be repeated in the new arrangement. Figure 2.21 demonstrates the computation of the median on a filter with a region of size 3×3.

Because a filter is normally defined as a matrix whose data set is odd, the median value always corresponds to the central value of the increasingly ordered vector corresponding to the region of interest $R(x,y)$.

It can be said that the median filter does not produce or calculate a new value with which the pixel of the image will be replaced, but rather this is an existing value in the region of interest of the filter selected as a result of data rearrangement. Figure 2.22 illustrates the effect of a median filter on two-dimensional structures. From the results of this figure, it can be seen in 2.22a and 2.22b that when the structures are smaller than half of the filter, they are removed. On the other hand, when they are equal to or larger than half, as in 2.22c and 2.22d, they remain practically unchanged. Figure 2.23 finally shows, using images, the effect of the median filter to remove distortions such as salt and pepper.

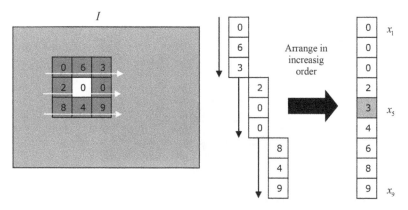

FIGURE 2.21
Calculation of the median considering a filter of size 3×3.

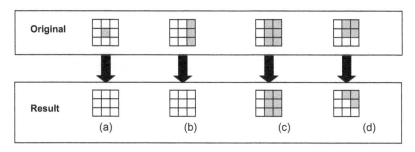

FIGURE 2.22
Effect of the median filter on structures can be seen in (a) and (b); when the structures are smaller than half the filter. They are eliminated, while when they are equal to or greater than half, as in (c) and (d), they remain practically unchanged.

2.8.3 Median Filter with Multiplicity Window

The median filter considers, in its determination, a set of data. Therefore, if there is a value with a very small or very large value compared to the other data that is covered by the region of interest $R(x,y)$ of the filter, it will not significantly alter the result. For this reason, the filter is very appropriate for removing salt and pepper noise.

With the median filter, all the pixels considered in the region of interest of the filter have the same importance in determining the result. As has been mentioned in several parts of this chapter, a desirable behavior in a filter would be to give greater weight to the central coefficient of the filter that corresponds to the pixel of the image to be replaced.

The median filter with a multiplicity window can be considered as a variant of the median filter, which, unlike the original, has a window H that gives different importance to each element depending on the corresponding

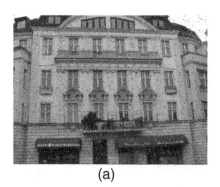

(a)

(b)

(c)

FIGURE 2.23

Results and comparison of the effect of the median filter. (a) The original image contaminated by salt and pepper noise (see Section 2.6). (b) Effect of the "Box" smoothing filter on the image (a). It can be seen how the filter is unable to eliminate the artifacts that distort the image; the only visible effect is their attenuation. (c) Median filter effect. It can be seen how this filter eliminates the noise present in the image.

coefficient of the filter matrix H. Thus, like linear filters, the matrix coefficients H scale their corresponding pixels in the image. However, the operation performed by this filter does not involve a multiplication of the filter coefficient by its corresponding pixel but multiplicity. In this context, it expresses the number of times the intensity value of the filter is presented where the median is calculated.

Under such conditions, the matrix of coefficients indicates in its total sum the number of data that are considered for the calculation of the median. Therefore, the size of the data T to be considered for the calculation of the median is distributed in a window of 3×3 considering the following matrix:

$$
H = \begin{bmatrix} h_1 & h_2 & h_3 \\ h_4 & h_5 & h_6 \\ h_7 & h_8 & h_9 \end{bmatrix} \tag{2.33}
$$

$$T = h_1 + h_2 + h_3 + h_4 + h_5 + h_6 + h_7 + h_8 + h_9$$

$$T = \sum_{i=1}^{9} h_i$$

As an example, consider if you have the filter H defined as:

$$H = \begin{bmatrix} 1 & 3 & 2 \\ 2 & 4 & 1 \\ 1 & 2 & 1 \end{bmatrix} \tag{2.34}$$

The data size T considered is as follows:

$$T = \sum_{i=1}^{9} h_i = 17 \tag{2.35}$$

Once the amount of data to be considered is known, the same method used in Section 2.6.2 is applied to find the median of the data set. Therefore, if the data set defined by T is odd, the median is the central data of the collection ordered in increasing order, but if it is even, then the average of the central data of the collection will have to be calculated as it is shown in Equation 2.31. Figure 2.24 illustrates the operation process of this filter.

Considering this method, the coefficients of the matrix H must be positive, and if the coefficient in a certain position is zero, it will be noted that this pixel of the image will not be considered for the determination of the median. An example of this is the median cross filter defined in Equation 2.33, which, as its name implies, considers only the cross of the coefficient matrix data.

$$H = \begin{bmatrix} 0 & 1 & 0 \\ 1 & 1 & 1 \\ 0 & 1 & 0 \end{bmatrix} \tag{2.36}$$

2.8.4 Other Non-Linear Filters

The median filter and its multiplicity window variant are just a few examples of non-linear filters that are frequently used and easy to explain. By the name of non-linear, we group all those filters that do not have the property of linearity. There are a large number of them that comply with the characteristic of nonlinearity. Some examples are the corner detector and the morphological filters that will be described in later chapters. An important difference

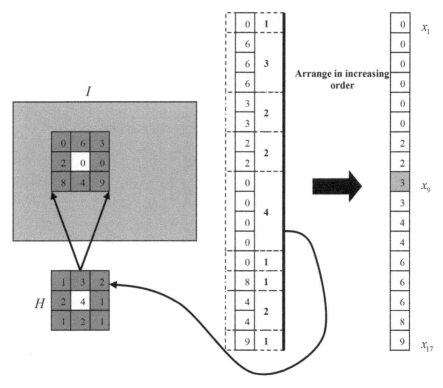

FIGURE 2.24
Calculation performed by the median filter with a multiplicity window of 3×3.

between non-linear filters is that the existing mathematical and theoretical basis for this type of filter is not the same as in the case of linear filters, which are based on convolution and their associated properties.

2.9 Linear Spatial Filters in MATLAB

To explain the options that MATLAB implements for spatial filtering, we analyze the way in which the correlation and convolution operations are carried out in detail. Then, we will see the possible functions available in order to implement such operations in MATLAB.

2.9.1 Correlation Size and Convolution

To exemplify the way in which these operations are carried out, the one-dimensional case is considered for simplicity. Therefore, it is assumed that there is a function f and a kernel k, as is shown in Figure 2.25a. For the correlation operation of a function and a kernel, we move both sequences in such a way that their reference points coincide, as shown in Figure 2.25b. From Figure 2.25b, it can be seen that there are coefficients that do not have a corresponding coefficient with which to interact. To solve this, the simplest thing is to add zeros at the beginning and at the end of the function f (see Figure 2.25c) so that during the displacement of the kernel. Therefore, a corresponding coefficient between both sequences is guaranteed.

The correlation operation is performed by shifting the kernel to the right, where the values of the correlation sequence at each step are obtained by adding the multiplicand values of the corresponding coefficients of both sequences. As Figure 2.25c shows, the result of the first element of the correlation sequence is zero. The last value of the correlation sequence is represented by the last geometric displacement achieved by the kernel on the function f, in such a way that the last value of the kernel corresponds to the

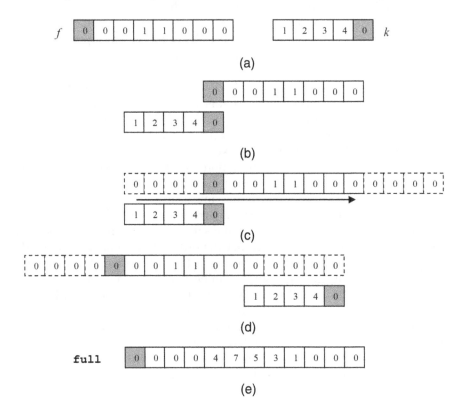

FIGURE 2.25
One-dimensional correlation operation performed between a function f and the kernel k. (a) Function and kernel, (b) alignment of both sequences at their reference point to perform correlation, (c) addition of zeros to the function to ensure correspondence of coefficients, (d) product between both sequences, and (e) 'full' result of the correlation.

last value of the original function of f (without adding zeros). This process is shown in Figure 2.25d.

If we execute the operation as described, the correlation sequence shown in Figure 2.25e will be obtained. It should be noted that if the reverse process is conducted, that is, the kernel is kept fixed and the displacement is carried out by the function f, the result would not be the same, so the order is important.

To use the functions implemented in MATLAB, it is important to associate the mathematical operations with the parameters used in their structure. Under such conditions, the correlation is considered 'full' if the operation is performed by moving the kernel k over the function f, with the addition of zeros.

Another alternative is to consider that the reference point is in the central coefficient of the kernel k. Therefore, the result will be equal to the size of the function f. This is because there will be fewer displacements between the kernel and the function. This type of operation is called 'same' in MATLAB. Figure 2.26 shows the process of correlation with this variant.

As a comparison, the same steps with which the 'full' correlation operation was developed are also established in Figure 2.26. An important thing to note is that the result of this correlation has the same size as the sequence of the function f.

In convolution, as already explained, a 180° rotation is verified on the kernel k. Then, the same process of correlation is applied. As with the correlation, the cases of 'full' and 'same' resulting from the operation are also applicable here. Thus, the operation will be 'full' or 'same' if it is used as a reference point, the initial coefficient of the kernel ('full') or the central coefficient ('same'). Figure 2.27 shows the computation process in the case of correlation.

From the figure, it is evident that rotating the kernel k by 180° reverses the reference point. The other steps are the same as those shown for the correlation case. Another important observation from the result of the convolution in its 'full' version is that it is exactly the same as that of the correlation for the same case, with the exception that the order of the sequence is exactly the opposite. Therefore, it is noted there is a close relationship between both operations. Similarly, the convolution can be calculated in its 'same' variant with the sole consideration that the kernel itself will have to be rotated. When it is inverted, it will change the order of the sequence but not the reference point. It is symmetric in relation to the two ends of the sequence remaining in the same position. This is illustrated in Figure 2.28.

The same concepts discussed here can be extended to the case of images. Figure 2.29 illustrates the correlation and convolution operations with their 'full' and 'same' variants.

2.9.2 Handling Image Borders

An important problem, as has been repeatedly mentioned in previous sections, is the way in which the limits of the image should be processed. When

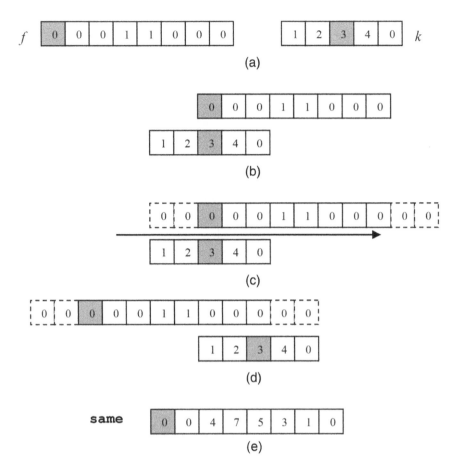

FIGURE 2.26
One-dimensional correlation operation performed between a function f and the kernel k considering that the reference point is the central coefficient of the kernel. (a) Function and kernel, (b) alignment of both sequences at their reference point to perform correlation, (c) addition of zeros to the function to ensure correspondence of coefficients, (d) product between both sequences, and (e) 'same' result of the correlation.

the correlation or convolution operation is applied to an image with a filter, there will be filter coefficients at the edges of the image that do not have a corresponding intensity value in the image. How this problem is treated has some effect on the final result.

There are four alternatives to solve this problem:

- Adding lines of zeros on the borders
- Replicating lines of values equal to the last rows or columns of the image.
- Adding the lines similar to if the image was reflected in a mirror.
- Adding lines as if the image repeats itself cyclically.

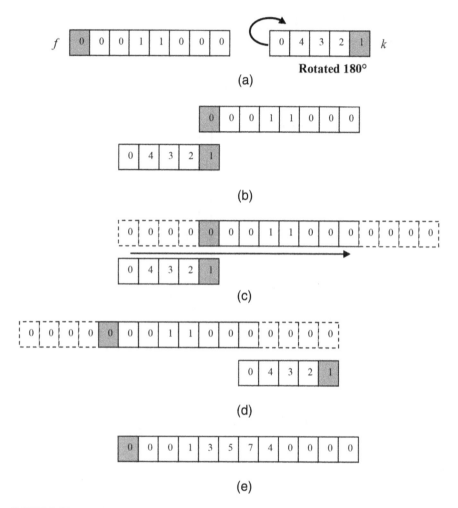

FIGURE 2.27
One-dimensional convolution operation performed between a function f and the kernel k rotated by 180°. (a) Function and kernel, (b) alignment of both sequences at their reference point to perform correlation, (c) addition of zeros to the function to ensure correspondence of coefficients, (d) product between both sequences, and (e) 'full' result of the correlation.

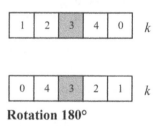

FIGURE 2.28
Rotation of the kernel to apply convolution.

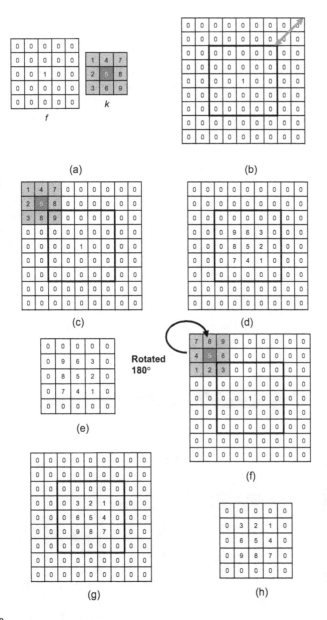

FIGURE 2.29

Correlation and convolution operations on images. (a) Original image *f* and kernel *k*, (b) original image to which "zeros" have been added in order to guarantee that there is an image value for each kernel coefficient, (c) start of the correlation of the kernel with the image to which zeros have been added, (d) result of the 'full' correlation, considering the image with the additional zeros, (e) result of the correlation of the same size 'same' as the image, without add zeros to the original image, it is the same size as the original, (f) original image and kernel rotated 180°, to convolve the image, (g) full result of the convolution, and (h) result of the convolution of the same size 'same' as the image.

Next, each of these elements will be briefly described. Then these concepts will also be associated with the way in which MATLAB incorporates such solutions into its functions.

Adding lines of zeros on the borders. This form has already been mentioned above as a solution to the border problem in images, in which lines of zeros are added, as many as necessary (depending on the size of the filter), to guarantee the coefficient-pixel correspondence. In MATLAB, this option to add zeros to the image is considered with the flag of '0'. Figure 2.30 illustrates this process.

Replicating lines of values equal to the last rows or columns of the image. In this option, lines are added to the image that are equal to the border lines of the image, which, in other words, would mean increasing the size of the image by repeating the last row or column of the image. They are integrated as many times as necessary (depending on filter size). This alternative is preferred over just adding zeros. In MATLAB, this option is defined by the 'replicate' flag. Figure 2.31 illustrates this process.

Adding the lines similar to if the image was reflected in a mirror. In this case, rows or columns are added to the image as if the image was reflected in a mirror at its borders. This option is a bit more complicated to implement than the previous ones since the rows or columns are not fixed like the previous ones but rather vary depending on how many it will be necessary to add

FIGURE 2.30
Adding zeros to the image in order to guarantee the correspondence of each filter coefficient per pixel of the image.

FIGURE 2.31
Add the last column or row, depending on the case, to the image in order to guarantee the correspondence of each filter coefficient per pixel of the image.

(depending on the size of the filter) to the image. In MATLAB, this option is defined by the 'symmetric' flag. Figure 2.32 illustrates this process.

Adding lines as if the image repeats itself cyclically. In this case, rows and columns are added to the image, considering it as if it were a signal that is repeated in all directions; that is, as if the image was spliced with an image above and below, on one side and on the other. In MATLAB, this option is defined by the 'circular' flag. Figure 2.33 illustrates this process.

2.9.3 MATLAB Functions for the Implementation of Linear Spatial Filters

The MATLAB image processing toolbox implements the function imfilter for linear spatial filtering of images, which has the following structure:

```
g=imfilter(f,H,filter_mode,border_options,result_size)
```

Where g is the filtered image and f is the image to be filtered with the filter H. The filters_mode flag specifies whether the function will use correlation ('corr') or convolution ('conv') for filtering. The border_options flag refers to the way in which the border problem will be solved by the function. The options are replicate, symmetric and circular, whose effects and implications were already discussed in Section, 2.8.2. The result_size flag indicates the size of the result obtained by the filter effect. Its options

FIGURE 2.32
Add columns or rows as appropriate to the image as if the image were reflected in a mirror at the borders of the image in order to guarantee the correspondence of each filter coefficient per pixel of the image.

can be same and full. Similarly, the effects of these options were already explained in Section 2.8.1. Table 2.1 shows a summary of the flags and their possible options.

As mentioned before, a convolution is the same as a correlation with the filter pre-rotated 180°. The opposite also applies. A correlation gives the same result as a convolution with the filter pre-rotated 180°. The above is important since the image processing toolbox defines several special filters that have been pre-rotated to be used directly with the correlation (default option) when they were originally planned to perform convolution on the image.

When we are working with a filter using convolution, there are two different options: one is to use the filter_mode (conv) flag of the imfilter function, and the other is to rotate the filter 180° and apply the imfilter function with its option default (corr). To rotate a matrix (in our case, a filter) with 180°, the following function can be used:

```
Hr=rot90(H,2)
```

where Hr is the filter rotated 180° and H is the filter to be rotated.

Figure 2.34 shows the use of the imfilter function and the effect of using the different options corresponding to the border_options flag,

FIGURE 2.33
Add columns or rows to the image as if the image were repeated cyclically on the borders in order to guarantee the correspondence of each filter coefficient per pixel of the image.

considering as filter H, a "Box" smoothing filter of 31 × 31, which was obtained by the following command in MATLAB:

```
H=ones(31,31)/(31*31);
```

As can be seen from Figure 2.34b, the `'0'` option when adding rows and columns with zeros produces a smoothing effect from black to white in regions where the original image does not have black pixels. The same happens in Figure 2.34e, where there are added equal rows and columns (`'circular'`) as if it were repeated above and below, on one side and on the other.

2.9.4 MATLAB Functions for Non-Linear Spatial Filtering

Non-linear filtering is based on the same mechanics as moving a mask along the image. However, unlike linear filtering, its operations do not consider the sum of multiplications between the filter coefficients and the image pixels. Another marked difference between linear and non-linear filtering is the role that plays the concept of masks or filter coefficients. In linear filters, filter coefficients determine the effect of the filter. On the other hand, in non-linear operations, the filter represents only the region of influence. Therefore, the mask symbolizes the pixels that will be considered in the processing and not the way in which they participate in the processing, as is the case in linear

TABLE 2.1

Summary of the Elements of the Structure from the imfilter Function

Options	Description
Filter mode	
corr	Filtering is implemented by using correlation. This option is used by default.
conv	Filtering is implemented by using convolution.
Border options	
0	The picture is completed by adding "zeros".
replicate	The image is completed by adding rows or columns that are equal to the border rows and columns of the image. It's the default option.
symetric	The image is completed with rows and columns equal to those obtained by mirror projection of the rows and columns of the reflected image.
circular	The image is completed with rows and columns equal to those obtained if the image is considered as a periodic signal, in such a way that the image is repeated above and below, on one side and on the other.
Result size	
full	The resulting filtered image is the size of the image with the columns and rows added at the borders to ensure pixel-coefficient correspondence.
same	The result of the filtered image is the size of the original image. It's the default option.

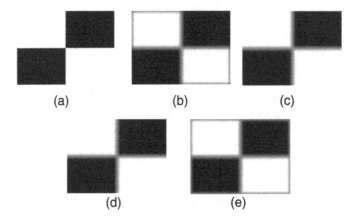

(a)   (b)   (c)

(d)   (e)

FIGURE 2.34
Effect of using the different options of the 'border_options' flag. (a) Original image, (b) effect on the image using the option '0', (c) effect on the image using the option 'replicate', (d) effect on the image using option 'symmetric', and (e) effect on image when using 'circular' option.

filtering. The image processing toolbox has two functions to perform non-linear filtering on images. These are: nlfilter and colfilt.

The nlfilter function allows filtering using a non-linear operation on an image. Its general syntax is:

```
B = nlfilter(A, [m n], @Fun);
```

where m and n determine the size of the region of influence of the non-linear filter that will be processed across the image. A corresponds to the image to be filtered, while B will contain the filtered image. fun defines a user function that implements the operation of the filter. This function receives from nlfilter a matrix of mxn data and returns the result of the non-linear operation implemented on that data. The @ symbol is called the function handle, which is a MATLAB data type that contains information about the function that is being used as a reference to implement the operation.

As an example, we will calculate the median filter using the nlfilter function. First, we need an image that contains salt and pepper noise. Therefore, considering the image exhibited in Figure 2.35a, salt and pepper-type noise is added at 10%, obtaining Figure 2.35b. This image has been produced using the following command:

(a)

(b)

(c)

FIGURE 2.35
Use of the nlfilter function. (a) Original image, (b) image distorted with salt and pepper noise, and (c) image filtered by nlfilter using the function defined in Program 2.3 that implements the median spatial non-linear filter.

```
Iruido=imnoise(I, 'salt & pepper', 0.1);
```

For the filtering, we will use a median filter defined by a neighborhood of 5×5. The operation (median) will be implemented using `nlfilter`, which will receive a matrix of 25 data. From these data, the median value is computed. The function created to implement this function is specified in Program 2.3. Once the function that will be used by the `nlfilter` function has been implemented, the image is filtered by using the following command:

```
R = nlfilter(Iruido, [5 5], @mediana);
```

PROGRAM 2.3. FUNCTION IMPLEMENTED TO FIND THE MEDIAN OF A DATA SET, WHICH ALLOWS IMPLEMENTING THE NON-LINEAR SPATIAL FILTER OF THE MEDIAN THROUGH THE MATLAB FUNCTION NLFILTER

```
%%%%%%%%%%%%%%%%%%%%%%%%%%%%%%%%%%%%%%%%%%%%%%%%%%%%%%%%%%%%%%%%
%%%%%
% Function to implement the non-linear median filter
using   %
% the nlfilter function
%
%%%%%%%%%%%%%%%%%%%%%%%%%%%%%%%%%%%%%%%%%%%%%%%%%%%%%%%%%%%%%%%%
%%%%%
% The function is created with the name with which it
% will be called, and it receives the vector x, which is
the
% pixels found in the region of influence mxn
function v=mediana(x)
% the median of the data set is found, and that data is
% delivered by the function
v=median(x(:));
```

Figure 2.35 illustrates the images used for the filtering performed by `nlfilter` and the effects obtained after this process.

The `colfilt` function performs the filtering by organizing the data in column form. This function is preferred over the `nlfilter` function since it achieves the calculation in a faster way.

Considering a region of interest $m \times n$, the `colfilt` function operates on an image I of size $M \times N$, generating a matrix A of size $mn \times MN$, in which each column corresponds to the pixels that form the area of interest centered on a position in the image. For example, the first column of matrix A involves the pixels that are part of the area of interest, centered on the pixel at the top left $(0,0)$ of the image I of dimension $M \times N$. The general syntax of this function is:

```
g=colfilt(I,[m n], 'sliding', @Fun);
```

where m and n represent the size of the considered region of interest or filter size. 'sliding' indicates that the mask $m \times n$ is displaced along the entire image I performing a pixel-by-pixel operation. fun defines a user function that implements the operation of the filter. This function receives from colfilt the matrix A of $mn \times MN$ and returns, as a result, a vector of $1 \times MN$ (the size of the image I) product of the implemented non-linear operation.

As an example, the median filter will be calculated again, but now with the colfilt function. As in the case of the nlfilter function, a filter with an area of interest of 5×5 is selected. The function must be implemented so that it receives an array of size $25 \times MN$ and return, as a result, a $1 \times MN$ vector representing the medians of all the pixels in the image where the mask of 5×5 has been centered. Program 2.4 shows the implementation of this function.

PROGRAM 2.4. THE FUNCTION IMPLEMENTED TO FIND THE MEDIAN OF A MATRIX A OF $mn \times MN$, WHICH ALLOWS IMPLEMENTING THE NON-LINEAR SPATIAL FILTER OF THE MEDIAN THROUGH THE MATLAB FUNCTION COLFILT

```
%%%%%%%%%%%%%%%%%%%%%%%%%%%%%%%%%%%%%%%%%%%%%%%%%%%%%%%%%%
%%%
% Function to implement the median non-linear filter
using
% the colfilt function
%%%%%%%%%%%%%%%%%%%%%%%%%%%%%%%%%%%%%%%%%%%%%%%%%%%%%%%%%%
%%%
%%%%%%%%%%%%%%%%%%%%%%%%%%%%%%%%%%%%%%%%%%%%%%%%%%%%%%%%%%
%%%
% The function is created with the name with which it
% will be called. It receives the matrix A of dimension
mnxMN
function v1=medianal(A)
% the median of each column of matrix A is found, which
is 25
% data (5x5) and returns a vector v1 of 1xMN with the
medians
% of the entire image, it will be the same with
median(A,1)
V1=median(A);
```

FIGURE 2.36
A binary image used to exemplify the operation of the binary filter.

a	b	c
d	*p*	e
f	g	h

FIGURE 2.37
Processing window used in the binary filter operation.

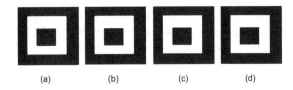

(a)   (b)   (c)   (d)

FIGURE 2.38
Binary filter operation. (a) Removal of black artifacts, (b) removal of white artifacts, (c) regeneration of corners of white elements, and (d) regeneration of corners on black objects.

2.10 Binary Filter

This filter is designed to work on binary images. It consists of a set of Boolean equations that allow for the removal of noise from white and black areas. The filter also has equations to reconstruct corners of figures that have degraded angles. In order to explain the operation of the filter equations, the binary image defined in Figure 2.36 is used as an example during the explanations.

Using the window 3×3 shown in Figure 2.37 as a processing reference, the new value P_0 will be obtained from p and pixels a, b, c, d, e, f, g, h that are its neighbors. The computation process is similar to that used in linear filters, with the exception that, in this case, logical operations are used. Therefore, the elements can only have values of True (1) and False (0).

The first step is to remove the noise or black artifacts from the white areas; for this propose, the following equation is used:

$$P_0 = p + \left(b \cdot g \cdot (d + e)\right) + \left(d \cdot e \cdot (b + g)\right) \tag{2.37}$$

The result of this processing is shown in Figure 2.38a. The second step is to remove the noise or white artifacts from the black areas, for which the equation is defined as follows:

$$P_0 = p \cdot \left(\left((a+b+d) \cdot (e+g+h) \right) + \left((b+c+e) \cdot (d+f+g) \right) \right) \quad (2.38)$$

The result of this process is shown in Figure 2.38b. To reconstruct the corners of the white figure, four different equations must be used, one for each corner of the figure. That is:
For the top right corner:

$$P_0 = \bar{p} \cdot d \cdot f \cdot g \cdot \overline{(a+b+c+e+h)} + p \quad (2.39)$$

For the lower right corner:

$$P_0 = \bar{p} \cdot a \cdot b \cdot d \cdot \overline{(c+e+f+g+h)} + p \quad (2.40)$$

For the top left corner:

$$P_0 = \bar{p} \cdot e \cdot g \cdot h \cdot \overline{(a+b+c+d+f)} + p \quad (2.41)$$

For the lower left corner:

$$P_0 = \bar{p} \cdot b \cdot c \cdot e \cdot \overline{(a+d+f+g+h)} + p \quad (2.42)$$

The result of these four operations is shown in Figure 2.38c. Finally, from the last four equations, another four equations are necessary for the regeneration of the corners in the black figures. They are defined as follows:
For the top right corner:

$$P_0 = p \cdot (d+f+g) + \overline{(a \cdot b \cdot c \cdot e \cdot h \cdot p)} \quad (2.43)$$

For the lower right corner:

$$P_0 = p \cdot (a+b+d) + \overline{(c \cdot e \cdot f \cdot g \cdot h \cdot p)} \quad (2.44)$$

For the top left corner:

$$P_0 = p \cdot (e+g+h) + \overline{(a \cdot b \cdot c \cdot d \cdot f \cdot p)} \quad (2.45)$$

For the lower left corner:

$$P_0 = p \cdot (b+c+e) + \overline{(a \cdot d \cdot f \cdot g \cdot h \cdot p)} \quad (2.46)$$

The result of these four operations, which define the final result of the binary filter processing, is shown in Figure 2.38d.

2.10.1 Implementation of the Binary Filter in MATLAB

This section shows how the binary filter can be implemented to operate on binary images. In the implementation of the filter, its operation was divided into four different functions, which must be applied sequentially.

The first function, called remove_black_noise removes artifacts or black points that are considered noise. This function is shown in Program 2.5.

PROGRAM 2.5. FUNCTION THAT ELIMINATES BLACK ARTIFACTS CONSIDERED NOISE AS PART OF THE BINARY FILTER OPERATION

```
%%%%%%%%%%%%%%%%%%%%%%%%%%%%%%%%%%%%%%%%%%%%%%%%%%%%%%%%%%%%%%
%%%%%%%%%%%%%%%
%
%
% Function to remove artifacts or black spots from a
%
% binary image, within the binary filter operation
%
%
%
%%%%%%%%%%%%%%%%%%%%%%%%%%%%%%%%%%%%%%%%%%%%%%%%%%%%%%%%%%%%%%
%%%%%%%%%%%%%%%
function Ifiltered = remove_black_noise(Ibin)
    Ifiltered = Ibin;
    % Get the size of the image
    [height, width] = size(Ifiltered);
    % The process is calculated for the entire image
    for m= 2: (height-1)
        for n= 2:  (width-1)
            % Binary pixels corresponding to a 3x3 mask
are obtained
            b= Ifiltered(m-1,n);
            d= Ifiltered(m,n-1);
            p= Ifiltered(m,n);
            e= Ifiltered(m,n+1);
            g= Ifiltered(m+1,n);
            % the Boolean equation defined in 2.38
applies
            Ifiltered(m,n)= p | (b&g&(d|e)) | (d&e&(b|g));
        end
    end
end
```

The function called `remove_white_point_noise` removes artifacts or white points that are considered noise. This function is shown in Program 2.6.

PROGRAM 2.6. FUNCTION THAT REMOVES WHITE ARTIFACTS CONSIDERED NOISE AS PART OF THE BINARY FILTER OPERATION

```
%%%%%%%%%%%%%%%%%%%%%%%%%%%%%%%%%%%%%%%%%%%%%%%%%%%%%%%%%%%%
%%%%%%%%%%%%%%%%
%
%
% Function to remove artifacts or white points from a
%
% binary image within the binary filter operation
%
%
%
%%%%%%%%%%%%%%%%%%%%%%%%%%%%%%%%%%%%%%%%%%%%%%%%%%%%%%%%%%%%
%%%%%%%%%%%%%%%%%
function Ifiltered = remove_white_point_noise(Ibin)
    Ifiltered = Ibin;
    % Get the size of the image
    [height, width] = size(Ifiltered);
    % The process is calculated for the entire image
    for m= 2: (height-1)
        for n= 2:  (width-1)
            % Binary pixels corresponding to a 3x3 mask
are obtained
            a= Ifiltered(m-1,n-1);
            b= Ifiltered(m-1,n);
            c= Ifiltered(m-1,n+1);
            d= Ifiltered(m,n-1);
            p= Ifiltered(m,n);
            e= Ifiltered(m,n+1);
            f= Ifiltered(m+1,n-1);
            g= Ifiltered(m+1,n);
            h= Ifiltered(m+1,n+1);
            % the boolean equation defined in 2.39
applies
            Ifiltered(m,n)= p & (((a|b|d)&(e|g|h)) |
((b|c|e)&(d|f|g)));
        end
    end
end
```

The function called `rebuild_white_corners` reestablishes the corners on white objects that have degraded angles. This function is shown in Program 2.7.

PROGRAM 2.7.   THE FUNCTION THAT RECONSTRUCTS THE CORNERS OF THE WHITE OBJECTS AS PART OF THE BINARY FILTER OPERATION

```
%%%%%%%%%%%%%%%%%%%%%%%%%%%%%%%%%%%%%%%%%%%%%%%%%%%%%%%%%%%%%%%%
%%%%%%%%%%%
%
%
% Function to reconstruct the corners of white objects
%
% that have defined angles, within the binary filter
operation      %
%
%
%%%%%%%%%%%%%%%%%%%%%%%%%%%%%%%%%%%%%%%%%%%%%%%%%%%%%%%%%%%%%%%%
%%%%%%%%%%%
function Ifiltered = rebuild_white_corners(Ibin)
    Ifiltered = Ibin;
    [height, width] = size(Ifiltered);
    for m= 2: (height-1)
        for n= 2:  (width-1)
        a= Ifiltered(m-1,n-1);
        b= Ifiltered(m-1,n);
        c= Ifiltered(m-1,n+1);
        d= Ifiltered(m,n-1);
        p= Ifiltered(m,n);
        e= Ifiltered(m,n+1);
        f= Ifiltered(m+1,n-1);
        g= Ifiltered(m+1,n);
        h= Ifiltered(m+1,n+1);
        % the logical equation defined in 2.40 applies
        Ifiltered(m,n)= ((not(p)) & (d&f&g) &
not(a|b|c|e|h))|p;
        end
    end
    for m= 2: (height-1)
        for n= 2:  (width-1)
        a= Ifiltered(m-1,n-1);
        b= Ifiltered(m-1,n);
        c= Ifiltered(m-1,n+1);
        d= Ifiltered(m,n-1);
        p= Ifiltered(m,n);
```

```
            e= Ifiltered(m,n+1);
            f= Ifiltered(m+1,n-1);
            g= Ifiltered(m+1,n);
            h= Ifiltered(m+1,n+1);
            % se aplica la ecuación lógica definida en 2.41
            Ifiltered(m,n)=((not(p))&(a&b&d)&(not(c|e|f|g|h))
)|p;
        end
    end
    for m= 2: (height-1)
        for n= 2:  (width-1)
            a= Ifiltered(m-1,n-1);
            b= Ifiltered(m-1,n);
            c= Ifiltered(m-1,n+1);
            d= Ifiltered(m,n-1);
            p= Ifiltered(m,n);
            e= Ifiltered(m,n+1);
            f= Ifiltered(m+1,n-1);
            g= Ifiltered(m+1,n);
            h= Ifiltered(m+1,n+1);
            % the logical equation defined in 2.42 applies
            Ifiltered(m,n)=((not(p))&(e&g&h)&(not(a|b|c|d|f))
)|p;
        end
    end
    for m= 2: (height-1)
        for n= 2: (width-1)
            a= Ifiltered(m-1,n-1);
            b= Ifiltered(m-1,n);
            c= Ifiltered(m-1,n+1);
            d= Ifiltered(m,n-1);
            p= Ifiltered(m,n);
            e= Ifiltered(m,n+1);
            f= Ifiltered(m+1,n-1);
            g= Ifiltered(m+1,n);
            h= Ifiltered(m+1,n+1);
            % the logical equation defined in 2.43 applies
            Ifiltered(m,n)=((not(p))&(b&c&e)&(not(a|d|f|g|h))
)|p;
        end
    end
end
```

The function called rebuild_black_corners reestablishes the corners on black objects that have defined angles. This function is shown in Program 2.8.

PROGRAM 2.8.　THE FUNCTION THAT RECONSTRUCTS THE CORNERS OF THE BLACK OBJECTS AS PART OF THE BINARY FILTER OPERATION

```
%%%%%%%%%%%%%%%%%%%%%%%%%%%%%%%%%%%%%%%%%%%%%%%%%%%%%%%%%%%%%%%%%
%%%%%%%%%
%
%
% Function to reconstruct the corners of black objects
%
% that have defined angles within the binary filter
operation     %
%
%
%%%%%%%%%%%%%%%%%%%%%%%%%%%%%%%%%%%%%%%%%%%%%%%%%%%%%%%%%%%%%%%%%
%%%%%%%%%
function Ifiltered = rebuild_black_corners(Ibin)
    Ifiltered = Ibin;
    [height, width] = size(Ifiltered);
    for m= 2: (height-1)
        for n= 2:  (width-1)
        a= Ifiltered(m-1,n-1);
        b= Ifiltered(m-1,n);
        c= Ifiltered(m-1,n+1);
        d= Ifiltered(m,n-1);
        p= Ifiltered(m,n);
        e= Ifiltered(m,n+1);
        f= Ifiltered(m+1,n-1);
        g= Ifiltered(m+1,n);
        h= Ifiltered(m+1,n+1);
        % the logical equation defined in 2.44 applies
        Ifiltered(m,n)= p& ( (d|f|g) + not(a&b&c&e&h&p)
);
        end
    end
    for m= 2: (height-1)
        for n= 2:  (width-1)
        a= Ifiltered(m-1,n-1);
        b= Ifiltered(m-1,n);
        c= Ifiltered(m-1,n+1);
        d= Ifiltered(m,n-1);
        p= Ifiltered(m,n);
        e= Ifiltered(m,n+1);
        f= Ifiltered(m+1,n-1);
        g= Ifiltered(m+1,n);
        h= Ifiltered(m+1,n+1);
        % the logical equation defined in 2.45 applies
```

```
            Ifiltered(m,n)= p & ( (a|b|d) | not(c&e&f&g&h&p)
);
        end
    end
    for m= 2: (height-1)
        for n= 2:  (width-1)
        a= Ifiltered(m-1,n-1);
        b= Ifiltered(m-1,n);
        c= Ifiltered(m-1,n+1);
        d= Ifiltered(m,n-1);
        p= Ifiltered(m,n);
        e= Ifiltered(m,n+1);
        f= Ifiltered(m+1,n-1);
        g= Ifiltered(m+1,n);
        h= Ifiltered(m+1,n+1);
        % the logical equation defined in 2.46 applies
        Ifiltered(m,n)= p & ( (e|g|h) + not(a&b&c&d&f&p)
);
        end
    end
    for m= 2: (height-1)
        for n= 2:  (width-1)
        a= Ifiltered(m-1,n-1);
        b= Ifiltered(m-1,n);
        c= Ifiltered(m-1,n+1);
        d= Ifiltered(m,n-1);
        p= Ifiltered(m,n);
        e= Ifiltered(m,n+1);
        f= Ifiltered(m+1,n-1);
        g= Ifiltered(m+1,n);
        h= Ifiltered(m+1,n+1);
        % the logical equation defined in 2.47 applies
        Ifiltered(m,n)= p & ( (b|c|e) | not(a&d&f&g&h&p)
) ;
        end
    end
end
```

References

[1] O'Regan, J. K. (2018). *Advanced digital image processing and analysis*. CRC Press.
[2] Acharya, T., & Ray, A. K. (2017). *Image processing: Principles and applications*. CRC Press.
[3] McAndrew, A. (2017). *Introduction to digital image processing with MATLAB*. CRC Press.
[4] Russ, J. C. (2011). *The image processing handbook* (6th ed.). CRC Press.

[5] Marques, O. (2011). *Practical image and video processing using MATLAB*. Wiley.

[6] Khatun, F., & Rahman, M. M. (2018). A Review of Edge Detection Techniques in Image Processing. Journal of Electromagnetic Analysis and Applications, 10(8), 206–214. https://doi.org/10.4172/2332-0796.1000150

[7] Umbaugh, S. E. (2017). *Digital image processing and analysis: Human and computer vision applications with CVIPtools* (2nd ed.). CRC Press.

[8] Demirkaya, O., & Asyali, M. H. (2016). *Image processing with MATLAB: Applications in medicine and biology*. CRC Press.

[9] Umbaugh, S. E. (2005). *Handbook of image processing and computer vision, Volume 1: Algorithms and techniques*. Wiley-Interscience.

3

Edge Detection

Features in an image, such as edges, are detected through local changes in intensity or color [1]. They play an important role in image interpretation. The subjective "clarity" of an image is directly related to the discontinuities and sharpness of the structures present in it. The human eye gives an important weight to the edges of objects since it is through these that a person can differentiate the different characteristics as well as the delimitations of the real forms. Therefore, simple traces on images are enough to interpret the classes of the objects. For this reason, edges are very important topics for digital image processing and machine vision.

3.1 Borders and Contours

Edges play a predominant role in human vision and probably also in other biological vision systems. The edges are not only noticeable, but it is also possible by means of a few edge lines to reconstruct the objects again (Figure 3.1). One of the main issues to be discussed is how edges originate in an image and how it is possible to locate them to be used in a post-processing stage.

Roughly, edges can be thought of as points in an image where the intensity in each direction changes dramatically [2]. Depending on the intensity change presented in a specific pixel, it will be the value of the edge in the image for that point. The size of the change is normally calculated from the

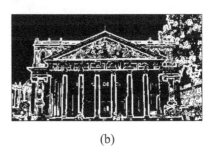

(a)   (b)

FIGURE 3.1
(a) Original image and (b) image with borders.

DOI: 10.1201/9781003287414-3

derivative and is used as one of the most important approaches to determining the edges of an image.

3.2 Edge Detection Using Gradient-Based Techniques

Consider a single dimension and take as an example an image that has a white region in the center surrounded by a dark background, like Figure 3.2a.

The grayscale profile along a line in the image might look like Figure 3.2b. We will define this one-dimensional signal as $f(u)$. Its first derivative is defined as follows:

$$f'(u) = \frac{df}{du}(u) \tag{3.1}$$

Thus, a positive elevation is produced in every place where the intensity increases and a negative one where the intensity decreases. However, the derivative is not defined for discrete functions such as $f(u)$, so we need a method to calculate it.

It is known that the derivative of a function at a point x can be interpreted by the slope of the tangent at that particular point. However, for a discrete function, the derivative at a point u (the slope of the tangent to that point) can be calculated from the difference between the neighboring points u divided

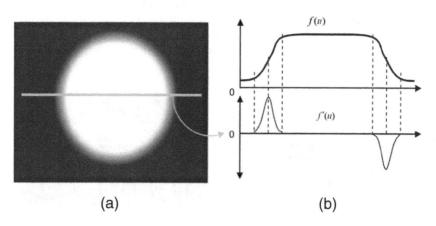

(a)   (b)

FIGURE 3.2
First derivative in the one-dimensional case obtained from the horizontal profile of the image. Original image (a) and the derivative of the horizontal profile obtained from the image (b).

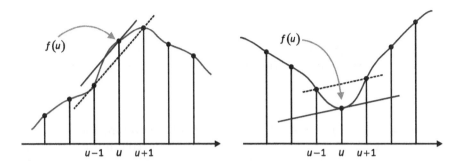

FIGURE 3.3
Calculation of the first derivative for a discrete function. The slope of the line through the neighboring points $f(u-1)$ and $f(u+1)$ is used as an indirect way to calculate the slope to the tangent at $f(u)$.

by the distant value between the two points [3], see Figure 3.3. So, the derivative can be approximated as follows:

$$\frac{df}{du}(u) \approx \frac{f(u+1)-f(u-1)}{2} = 0.5 \cdot \left(f(u+1)-f(u-1)\right) \tag{3.2}$$

The same process can also be used for the vertical direction along the column of the image.

3.2.1 Partial Derivative and Gradient

The partial derivative can be thought of as the derivative of a multidimensional function along a coordinate axis (with respect to one of the function variables), for example:

$$\frac{\partial I(x,y)}{\partial x} \text{ and } \frac{\partial I(x,y)}{\partial y} \tag{3.3}$$

The partial derivative of the image function $I(u,v)$ with respect to the variable u or v can be defined as the following vector:

$$\nabla I(x,y) = \begin{bmatrix} \dfrac{\partial I(x,y)}{\partial x} \\ \dfrac{\partial I(x,y)}{\partial y} \end{bmatrix} \tag{3.4}$$

This formulation represents the gradient vector of function I at the point (x,y). The value of the gradient is modeled as follows:

$$|\nabla I| = \sqrt{\left(\frac{\partial I}{\partial x}\right)^2 + \left(\frac{\partial I}{\partial y}\right)^2} \tag{3.5}$$

The value of $|\nabla I|$ is invariant to image rotations and thus also independent of the orientation of the structures contained in it. This property is important for locating the edge points of the image; thus, the value of $|\nabla I|$ is the practical value used in most of the algorithms considered for edge detection.

3.2.2 Derived Filter

The components of the gradient in Equation 3.4 are nothing more than the first derivative, both in the sense of the rows and the columns of the image. According to Figures 3.2 and 3.3, the derivative in the horizontal direction is computed as a filter operation with the following matrix of coefficients:

$$H_x^D = \begin{bmatrix} -0.5 & \underline{0} & 0.5 \end{bmatrix} = 0.5 \cdot \begin{bmatrix} -1 & \underline{0} & 1 \end{bmatrix} \tag{3.6}$$

where the coefficient -0.5 affects the pixel $I(x-1,y)$ and 0.5 affects the pixel $I(x+1,y)$. The value of the middle pixel $I(x,y)$ is multiplied by zero or equally ignored (here, the element under which the underscore "_" is considered to represent the reference point or the pixel under which the property in question is calculated). In the same way, the same effect of the filter can be established, but now in the vertical direction, being its matrix of coefficients:

$$H_y^D = \begin{bmatrix} -0.5 \\ \underline{0} \\ 0.5 \end{bmatrix} = 0.5 \cdot \begin{bmatrix} -1 \\ 0 \\ 1 \end{bmatrix} \tag{3.7}$$

Figure 3.4 shows the effect of applying the filters defined in Equations 3.6 and 3.7 on an image. The dependency on direction presented in Figure 3.4 is easy to recognize. The horizontal gradient filter H_x^D reacts, resulting in a larger response in the horizontal direction and highlighting the edges in the vertical direction [Figure 3.4b]. In the same way, the H_y^D filter acts, causing particularly large values in the vertical direction, thereby enhancing the horizontal edges of a structure [Figure 3.4c]. In the regions of the image where the filter response was null [in Figures 3.4b and c], the values were represented by gray pixels.

3.3 Filters for Edge Detection

The way of computing the local gradient corresponding to each pixel of the image is what fundamentally differentiates each of the operators for edge detection. The main difference is that the gradient is calculated as distinct

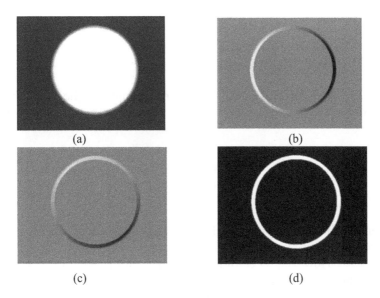

(a) (b)

(c) (d)

FIGURE 3.4
The first partial derivatives. (a) Synthetic image, (b) first partial derivative on the horizontal direction $\partial I/\partial u$, (c) on the vertical direction $\partial I/\partial v$, (d) value of the gradient $|\nabla I|$. In (b) and (c) are the dark values belonging to negative values, the brightest values belonging to positive values, while gray corresponds to zero.

directional components. Likewise, the partial results (obtained by each direction) are joined into a final one. In the computation of the gradient, we are interested not only in the value of the gradient in a pixel but also in the direction of the edge in question. However, as both elements (gradient value and direction) are implicit in the gradient calculation, it is possible to obtain them easily [4]. Some of the best-known edge operators will be presented below, either because of their practical application or because they have been historically interesting.

3.3.1 Prewitt and Sobel Operators

The Prewitt and Sobel operators represent two of the most used methods in edge detection [5], which are very similar to each other, differing only by some details.

3.3.1.1 The Filter

Both operators use a 3×3 coefficient matrix as a filter. This size and configuration allow the filter to be less prone to its own noise compared to the filters presented in Equations 3.6 and 3.7. The Prewitt operator uses the filter defined by

$$H_x^P = \begin{bmatrix} -1 & 0 & 1 \\ -1 & 0 & 1 \\ -1 & 0 & 1 \end{bmatrix} \text{ y } H_y^P = \begin{bmatrix} -1 & -1 & -1 \\ 0 & 0 & 0 \\ 1 & 1 & 1 \end{bmatrix} \qquad (3.8)$$

These filters are obviously applied to the different neighbors of the pixel in question. If the filters are analyzed in their separate forms, we have the following:

$$H_x^P = \begin{bmatrix} 1 \\ 1 \\ 1 \end{bmatrix} * \begin{bmatrix} -1 & 0 & -1 \end{bmatrix} \text{ o bien } H_y^P = \begin{bmatrix} 1 & 1 & 1 \end{bmatrix} * \begin{bmatrix} -1 \\ 0 \\ -1 \end{bmatrix} \qquad (3.9)$$

Each one of the vectors on the right, either in the case of H_x^P or H_y^P produces three columns or rows that constitute the coefficients of the filter defined in equation 3.8. However, as can be seen, this vector $\begin{bmatrix} -1 & 0 & -1 \end{bmatrix}$ maintains the derivative approximation defined in Section 3.2.2. It is also possible to notice how the vector on the left $\begin{bmatrix} 1 & 1 & 1 \end{bmatrix}$ in both cases implies a data smoothing operation, thus showing how, apart from locating or enhancing the pixels belonging to the edges, the filter performs a smoothing operation. This makes the filter more robust to the noise presented in the image.

The Sobel operator has practically an identical filter to the Prewitt operator, with the only difference being that in this filter, greater weight is given to the central row or column of the filter. The coefficient matrix for this operator is defined as follows:

$$H_x^S = \begin{bmatrix} -1 & 0 & 1 \\ -2 & 0 & 2 \\ -1 & 0 & 1 \end{bmatrix} \text{ y } H_y^S = \begin{bmatrix} -1 & -2 & -1 \\ 0 & 0 & 0 \\ 1 & 2 & 1 \end{bmatrix} \qquad (3.10)$$

The results of the Prewitt and Sobel filters produce estimates of the local gradient for all the pixels of the image in their two different directions, maintaining the following relationship:

$$\nabla I(x,y) \approx \frac{1}{6} \begin{bmatrix} H_x^P \cdot I \\ H_y^P \cdot I \end{bmatrix} \text{ y } \nabla I(x,y) \approx \frac{1}{8} \begin{bmatrix} H_x^S \cdot I \\ H_y^S \cdot I \end{bmatrix} \qquad (3.11)$$

3.3.1.2 Gradient Size and Direction

Regardless of if it is a Prewitt or Sobel operator, the results of the filters for each of the different directions will be characterized as follows:

$$D_x(x,y) = H_x * I \text{ y } D_y(x,y) = H_y * I \qquad (3.12)$$

The magnitude of the edge $E(u,v)$ is, in both cases, defined as the magnitude of the gradient:

$$E(x,y) = \sqrt{(D_x(x,y))^2 + (D_y(x,y))^2} \tag{3.13}$$

The direction of the gradient at each pixel (the angle) is calculated as follows (Figure 3.5):

$$\phi(x,y) = \tan^{-1}\left(\frac{D_y(x,y)}{D_x(x,y)}\right) \tag{3.14}$$

The computation of the gradient direction using the Prewitt operator and the original version of the Sobel operator is relatively imprecise. Therefore, it is suggested that instead of using the Sobel filter presented in Equation 3.10, employ the version that minimizes the angle error, defined by:

$$H_x^{S'} = \frac{1}{32}\begin{bmatrix} -3 & 0 & 3 \\ -10 & 0 & 10 \\ -3 & 0 & 3 \end{bmatrix} \text{ and } H_y^{S'} = \frac{1}{32}\begin{bmatrix} -3 & -10 & -3 \\ 0 & 0 & 0 \\ 3 & 10 & 3 \end{bmatrix} \tag{3.15}$$

Due to its good results and simple implementation, the Sobel operator is widely used and employed in most commercial software packages used for digital image processing (Figure 3.6).

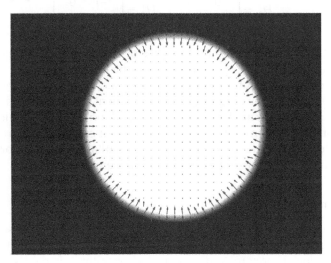

FIGURE 3.5
Representation of the magnitude of the gradient $E(x,y)$ and its direction $\phi(x,y)$. The complete process for edge detection is again summarized in Figure 3.6. First, the original image is filtered through the two coefficient matrices H_x and H_y, and consequently, their results are gathered in the magnitude of the gradient $E(x,y)$ and in the direction of the same $\phi(x,y)$.

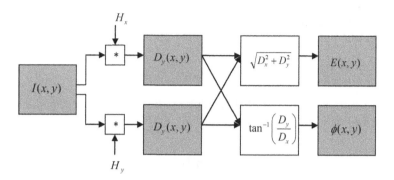

FIGURE 3.6

Typical operation of filters used for edge detection. With both coefficient matrices H_x and H_y, the gradient images D_x and D_x are produced, and with them the magnitude of the gradient $E(x,y)$ and $\phi(x,y)$ its direction are also calculated.

3.3.2 The Roberts Operator

The Roberts operator is one of the oldest filters used for locating edges in an image [6]. In this section, it will be described. A particularity of this filter is that it is extremely small, using only a 2×2 coefficient matrix to determine the gradient in its two different directions along its diagonals. The operator is defined as follows:

$$H_1^R = \begin{bmatrix} 0 & 1 \\ -1 & 0 \end{bmatrix} \quad H_2^R = \begin{bmatrix} -1 & 0 \\ 0 & 1 \end{bmatrix} \tag{3.16}$$

This filter reacts particularly to the edges of the image that have a diagonal direction (Figure 3.7). However, this makes the filter not very selective in the direction of the gradient, mainly when it is calculated on regions with different orientations. The magnitude of the gradient is calculated as defined in Equation 3.5, considering both components H_1^R and H_2^R. Nevertheless, due to the diagonal operation of the filter on the data, it can be considered that the magnitude of the gradient is formed as the resultant of two vectors (H_1^R and H_2^R) that are at 45°. Figure 3.8 illustrates this operation.

3.3.3 Compass Operators

A problem in the design of filters for edge detection is that the more sensitive the detection of the edge of a structure is preferred, the more dependent it becomes on its direction. Therefore, to design a good operator, it is necessary to make a trade-off between response magnitude and sensitivity to gradient direction.

A solution for this is not to use only two filters that break down the filter action in two directions, either horizontally and vertically in the case of the Prewitt and Sobel operators or diagonally up or down as it is for the

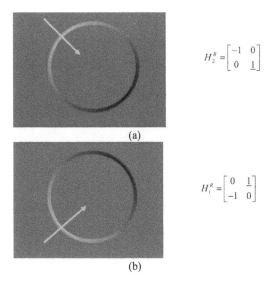

$$H_2^R = \begin{bmatrix} -1 & 0 \\ 0 & 1 \end{bmatrix}$$

(a)

$$H_1^R = \begin{bmatrix} 0 & 1 \\ -1 & 0 \end{bmatrix}$$

(b)

FIGURE 3.7
Diagonal components of the Roberts operator: (a) component H_2^R and (b) component H_1^R. From the images, it is easy to recognize the directional character in the calculation of this operator to find the magnitude of the gradient in each pixel of the image.

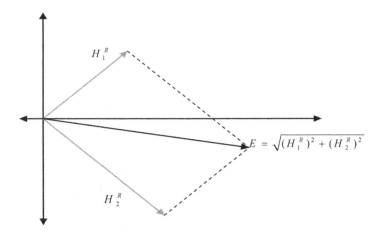

$$E = \sqrt{(H_1^R)^2 + (H_2^R)^2}$$

FIGURE 3.8
The magnitude of the gradient considering the Roberts operator. The magnitude of the gradient $E(x, y)$ is calculated as the sum of the two orthogonal filters H_1^R and H_2^R, that are applied for each direction of the diagonal.

Roberts operator, but to use filters for a larger number of directions. A classic example is the Kirsch operator, which consists of eight different filters, each one separated from the other by 45°. Therefore, it covers all directions for efficient edge detection. The coefficient matrices of this operator are defined as follows:

$$H_0^K = \begin{bmatrix} -1 & 0 & 1 \\ -2 & 0 & 2 \\ -1 & 0 & 1 \end{bmatrix}, H_1^K = \begin{bmatrix} -2 & -1 & 0 \\ -1 & 0 & 1 \\ 0 & 1 & 2 \end{bmatrix},$$

$$H_2^K = \begin{bmatrix} -1 & -2 & -1 \\ 0 & 0 & 0 \\ -1 & 0 & 1 \end{bmatrix}, H_3^K = \begin{bmatrix} 0 & -1 & -2 \\ 1 & 0 & -1 \\ 2 & 1 & 0 \end{bmatrix}$$

(3.17)

From these eight filters $H_0^K, H_1^K, ..., H_7^K$, only four must be calculated since the last four are equal to the first four except for the sign. For example, $H_4^K = -H_0^K$. Due to the linearity property of convolution, it is clear that

$$I * H_4^K = I * -H_0^K = -\left(I * H_0^K \right)$$

(3.18)

The images produced by the operation of the Kirsch filters $D_0, D_1, ..., D_7$ are generated in the following way:

$$D_0 = I * H_0^K \quad D_1 = I * H_1^K \quad D_2 = I * H_2^K \quad D_3 = I * H_3^K$$

$$D_4 = -D_0 \quad D_5 = -D_1 \quad D_6 = -D_2 \quad D_7 = -D_3$$

(3.19)

The magnitude of the gradient, which can be conceived as a composition of all the images produced by the Kirsch filters, is calculated in the pixel (x, y) as the maximum of the values of the images obtained by the operation of each of the eight filters. So, the value of the magnitude of the gradient for the pixel (x, y) is defined as follows:

$$E^K(x, y) = \max\left(D_0(x, y), D_1(x, y), ..., D_7(x, y) \right)$$

$$= \max\left(|D_0(x, y)|, |D_1(x, y)|, ..., |D_3(x, y)| \right)$$

(3.20)

The direction of the gradient is determined by the filter that presents the maximal contribution in the calculation of the magnitude of the gradient. Therefore, the direction of the gradient is specified as follows:

$$\phi^K(x, y) = \frac{\pi}{4} l \text{ where } l = \underset{0 \leq i \leq 7}{\operatorname{argmax}} \left(D_i(x, y) \right)$$

(3.21)

3.3.4 Edge Detection with MATLAB®

Considering the previous sections as theoretical foundations, this section presents how we can use MATLAB to calculate the edges of an image. To generate programs that allow finding edges of an image using any of the

Sobel, Prewitt, Roberts, or Kirsch operators, it is necessary to divide the program into three parts.

In the first part, it is necessary to generate one image per filter. Normally, there are two images that correspond to the different directions in which the operator is defined (see Equation 3.4). In this part, the filter, which is a matrix of coefficients, is spatially convolved with the original image. The result of this process is the magnitude values of the gradient in the direction defined for each filter. Figure 3.9 shows this process, considering the Sobel operator.

In the second part, the magnitude of the gradient is obtained from the resulting images from the convolution process between the filter (either horizontal or vertical) and the image (see Equation 3.5).

In the third part, a threshold **U** is set that characterizes the value from which the pixel in question is considered to be part of an edge. This value naturally defines the structural properties of the objects. By using this threshold **U**, the image with the gradient magnitudes is binarized. The elements in this image present only ones and zeros. A pixel will be one if it is an edge. Otherwise, it will be zero. Program 3.1 shows the MATLAB implementation for determining the edges in an image, considering the Sobel operator as the operator.

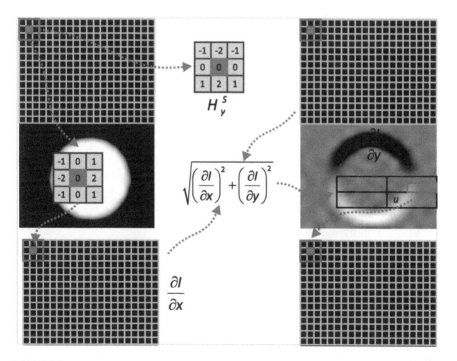

FIGURE 3.9
The implementation process for determining the magnitude of the gradient using the Sobel operator.

PROGRAM 3.1. DETERMINING THE BORDERS
OF AN IMAGE WITH MATLAB

```
%%%%%%%%%%%%%%%%%%%%%%%%%%%%%%%%%%%%%%%%%%%%%%%%%%%%%%%%%%%%%%%
%%%%%%
% Determining the Edges of an Image Using the Sobel
Operator %
%%%%%%%%%%%%%%%%%%%%%%%%%%%%%%%%%%%%%%%%%%%%%%%%%%%%%%%%%%%%%%%
%%%%%%
% The original image is brought into the MATLAB
environment
I=imread('fotos/puente.jpg');
% Convert the original image to an intensity image
% to be able to operate on it
Im=rgb2gray(I);
% The values of the dimensions of the image are obtained
[m,n]=size(Im);
% The image is converted to double to avoid problems
% in data type conversion
Im=double(Im);
% Matrices are created with zeros
Gx=zeros(size(Im));
Gy=zeros(size(Im));

% FIRST PART
% Sobel Filters (see Equation 6.10) are applied
% to the image Gx, in the x-direction and
% Gy in the y-direction
for r=2:m-1
    for c=2:n-1
        Gx(r,c)=-1*Im(r-1,c-1)-2*Im(r-1,c)-Im(r-1,c+1)...
            +Im(r+1,c-1)+2*Im(r+1,c)+Im(r+1,c+1);
        Gy(r,c)=-1*Im(r-1,c-1)+Im(r-1,c+1)-2*Im(r,c-1)...
            +2*Im(r,c+1)-Im(r+1,c-1)+Im(r+1,c+1);
    end
end

% SECOND PART
% Total Gradient Value is calculated
% (see Equation 3.5 or 3.13)
Gt=sqrt(Gx.^2+Gy.^2);
% The maximum value of the gradient is obtained
VmaxGt=max(max(Gt));
% Normalize the gradient to 255
GtN=(Gt/VmaxGt)*255;

% The image is converted for display
GtN=uint8(GtN);
```

```
% The minimum values for the Gradients x and y are
obtained.
VminGx=min(min(Gx));
VminGy=min(min(Gy));

% Using the lows shifts to avoid negatives.
GradOffx=Gx-VminGx;
GradOffy=Gy-VminGy;

% The maximum values for Gx and Gy are obtained.
VmaxGx=max(max(GradOffx));
VmaxGy=max(max(GradOffy));

% Gradients are normalized to 255
GxN=(GradOffx/VmaxGx)*255;
GyN=(GradOffy/VmaxGy)*255;

% The image is converted for display
GxN=uint8(GxN);
GyN=uint8(GyN);

% Display of the gradients in x and y
figure
imshow(GxN)
figure
imshow(GyN)

% THIRD PART
% The image is binarized considering a threshold of 100
B=GtN>25;
% Full gradient display
figure
imshow(GtN)
% Edge Image Display
figure
imshow(B)
```

The results of the code shown in Program 3.1 are shown in Figure 3.10, where it is possible to observe the original intensity image, the gradients obtained by the Sobel operator on the *x*-axis, on the *y*-axis, as well as the total gradient and the edges.

3.3.5 MATLAB Functions for Edge Detection

The image processing toolbox provides the function edge, which implements the different operators discussed in the previous sections (Sobel, Prewitt, and Roberts) [7]. For some of these operators, it is also possible to

FIGURE 3.10
Results of applying the code described in Program 3.1 on an intensity image, (a) original gray-scale image, (b) gradient in x, (c) gradient in y, (d) total gradient, and (e) image of borders.

specify the direction of the filter to calculate. Therefore, it can be indicated by the sensitivity with which the computation of the gradient in horizontal, vertical, or both directions is performed. The general structure of the function is described as follows:

```
[g,t]=edge(f, 'method', parameters)
```

where f is the image from which the edges are extracted. method corresponds to one of the operators listed in Table 3.1. parameters represent the specifications that must be configured depending on the type of method used. The output g is a binary image where the pixels belonging

TABLE 3.1

Edge Detection Operators Used by the Edge Function of the Image Processing Toolbox.

Operator	'method'	Filters	
Prewitt	'prewitt'	$$H_y^P = \begin{bmatrix} -1 & -1 & -1 \\ 0 & 0 & 0 \\ 1 & 1 & 1 \end{bmatrix}$$	$$H_y^P = \begin{bmatrix} -1 & -1 & -1 \\ 0 & 0 & 0 \\ 1 & 1 & 1 \end{bmatrix}$$
Sobel	'sobel'	$$H_x^S = \begin{bmatrix} -1 & 0 & 1 \\ -2 & 0 & 2 \\ -1 & 0 & 1 \end{bmatrix}$$	$$H_y^S = \begin{bmatrix} -1 & -2 & -1 \\ 0 & 0 & 0 \\ 1 & 2 & 1 \end{bmatrix}$$
Roberts	'roberts'	$$H_1^R = \begin{bmatrix} 0 & \bar{1} \\ -1 & 0 \end{bmatrix}$$	$$H_2^R = \begin{bmatrix} -1 & 0 \\ 0 & \bar{1} \end{bmatrix}$$

to the detected edges of f have a value of 1. Otherwise, they have a value of zero. The t parameter is optional and provides the threshold used by the algorithm to determine which value of the gradient can be considered as an edge.

3.3.5.1 Sobel Operator

The Sobel operator uses the filters described in Table 3.1 to approximate the partial derivatives $\partial I/\partial u$ and $\partial I/\partial v$. From the combination of these partial derivatives according to Equation 3.5, we obtain each pixel (u,v) the gradient value. Then, a pixel (u,v) is said to correspond to an edge of the image if the value of its gradient is greater than a pre-established threshold **U** as a criterion.

The general call to the edge detection function that the image processing toolbox implements under the Sobel method is:

```
[g,t]=edge(f, 'sobel', U, dir)
```

where f is the image from which the edges will be extracted. U is a threshold that is used as the criterion to classify the edges. dir selects the direction of the gradient, which can be 'horizontal' if used H_x^S or 'vertical' if H_y^S is used. The option 'both', which is the default option, implies the calculation of both filters. As a result, the function obtains the image g, which, as stated above, contains the detected edges. g is a binary image where the edge pixels have the value of 1, while not edge pixels present the value of zero. If the threshold U is specified t = U. If U is not specified, the algorithm automatically determines one, uses it for edge detection, and returns its value in t.

3.3.5.2 Prewitt Operator

The Prewitt operator uses the coefficient matrices specified in Table 3.1 for edge detection. The general structure of this function is described as follows:

```
[g,t]=edge(f, 'prewitt', U, dir)
```

The parameters of this function are identical to those indicated in the Sobel case. The Prewitt operator is a little simpler (computationally speaking) in its implementation in relation to the Sobel case. Nevertheless, the results obtained are noisier. This is because the Sobel filter performs a smoothing operation on the data, which can be observed in the coefficients with value two in the row or column of the pixel on which the gradient is calculated.

3.3.5.3 Roberts Operator

The Roberts operator uses the filters defined in Table 3.1 to approximate the gradient magnitude at the pixel (u, v). The general structure of this function is described as follows:

```
[g,t]=edge(f, 'roberts', U, dir)
```

The parameters of this function are identical to those described in the case of the Sobel operator. The Roberts operator represents one of the oldest methods for calculating the gradient in images. Although this method is the simplest to implement, it has limited functionality since it is non-symmetric. Therefore, it cannot detect edges that are directionally in multiples of 45°. As a comparison, Figure 3.11 shows the result of applying the previous functions to each of the different operators to detect the edges in an image. In the figure, all the functions use the same threshold for all cases.

3.4 Operators Based on the Second Derivative

Previously, the group of operators based on the first derivative has been described in Section 3.2 as a way of approximating the gradient of the image. In addition to these filters, there are other types of operators that are based on the second derivative of the image function [8]. In an image, intensity changes can be calculated by the value of the derivative in each direction (maximum gradient) or by the zero crossing of the second derivative (Laplacian) in any direction. As can be seen, the problem of using the first derivative as an approach for edge detection results in its difficult location when representing a highly directional method or when the edge is not well defined.

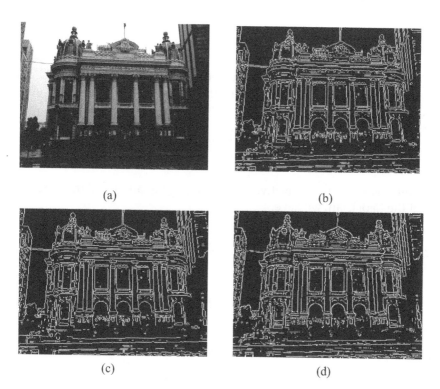

(a)   (b)

(c)   (d)

FIGURE 3.11

Comparison of the different operators used for edge detection. (a) Original image, (b) edges detected by the Sobel operator, (c) Prewitt, and (d) Roberts. In all cases, a U = 0.05 has been used.

Although the value of the gradient allows the detection of an edge, it is sometimes important to have information about whether the pixel presents a positive or negative transition of the gradient. This is equivalent to knowing if the pixel is on the dark or light side of the edge.

3.4.1 Edge Detection Using the Second-Derivative Technique

This technique is based on finding what is called zero-crossing. A zero crossing is nothing more than the transition from positive to negative or vice versa and is estimated from the second derivative.

The definition of a derivative for a one-dimensional function is as follows:

$$\frac{\partial f}{\partial x} = f(x+1) - f(x) \tag{3.22}$$

Likewise, from Equation 3.22, it can be said that the second derivative is defined as:

$$\frac{\partial f^2}{\partial x^2} = f(x+1) - 2f(x) + f(x-1) \tag{3.23}$$

The detection of edges by means of the second derivative is based on the zero crossing of the value of the gradient in any direction. To produce this effect, we use the Laplacian, which is insensitive to rotation and isotropic.

$$\nabla^2 I(x,y) = \frac{\partial^2 I(x,y)}{\partial x^2} + \frac{\partial^2 I(x,y)}{\partial y^2} \tag{3.24}$$

This filter uses second derivatives. Considering Equation 3.23 in expression 3.24 of the Laplacian, we have:

$$\frac{\partial^2 I(x,y)}{\partial x^2} = I(x+1,y) - 2I(x,y) + I(x-1,y) \tag{3.25}$$

$$\frac{\partial^2 I(x,y)}{\partial y^2} = I(x,y+1) - 2I(x,y) + I(x,y-1) \tag{3.26}$$

Therefore, if the expressions 3.25 and 3.26 are replaced in 3.24, we have:

$$\nabla^2 I(x,y) = I(x+1,y) + I(x-1,y)$$
$$+ I(x,y+1) + I(x,y-1) - 4I(x,y) \tag{3.27}$$

If the previous equation is expressed in terms of a filter, the matrix coefficients are defined as those shown in Figure 3.12.

An example of the application of the Laplacian filter on a grayscale image is shown in Figure 3.14. It presents the different effects of applying the double derivative in each of the directions and, finally, the result of the sum of the two, as the Laplacian is defined. The equation defined in 3.27 and expressed in the form of a filter in Figure 3.12 does not consider the variations in the diagonal neighbors of the pixel in question, which can be incorporated into the filter, with the consideration that by doing this, we will increase the

0	1	0
1	-4	1
0	1	0

FIGURE 3.12
Filter that represents the calculation of the Laplacian on an image, obtained from Equation 3.23

number of ones by 4 contained in the filter. Therefore, the central coefficient will have to be increased to 8. Considering the above, the Laplacian filter would be defined as described in Figure 3.13.

As can be seen from the calculation of the Laplacian filters, they have a response of zero in uniform grayscale regions and different for regions with varying grayscales. This is since these types of filters behave like high-pass filters. The sum of the coefficients is always zero (Figure 3.14).

1	1	1
1	-8	1
1	1	1

FIGURE 3.13
Laplacian filter with the extension of the diagonal neighbors to the central pixel

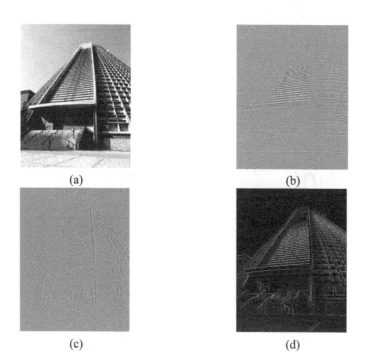

(a)

(b)

(c)

(d)

FIGURE 3.14
Use of the Laplacian filter. (a) Original figure, (b) horizontal second-order partial derivative $\partial^2 I(x,y)/\partial x^2$, (c) vertical second-order partial derivative $\partial^2 I(x,y)/\partial y^2$, and (d) the Laplacian operator $\nabla^2 I(x,y)$

3.4.2 Sharpness Enhancement in Images

If the Laplacian operator is applied to an image, we will obtain its edges. However, if what is desired is to improve the sharpness of an image, then it will be necessary to preserve the low-frequency information of the original image and emphasize the details present in the image through the Laplacian filter. To achieve this effect, it is necessary to subtract from the original image a scaled version of the Laplacian filter value. So, the image with improved sharpness would be defined as described in the following equation:

$$I(x,y)_{\text{Enhanced}} = I(x,y) - w \cdot \nabla^2 I(x,y) \tag{3.28}$$

Figure 3.15 shows the concept by which the image improves its sharpness by making the presence of its edges more prominent. To facilitate the explanation, the figure considers only the one-dimensional case.

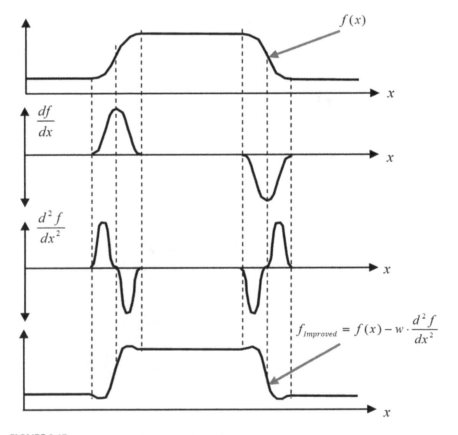

FIGURE 3.15
Sharpening by applying the second derivative. By subtracting a factor from the second derivative of the function, it is possible to maximize the presence of the borders in the image.

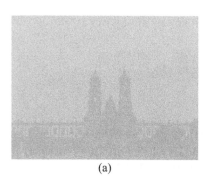 

(a)   (b)

FIGURE 3.16
Application of the Laplacian filter to improve the sharpness of an image. (a) Original image and (b) the image resulting from applying $I(x,y)_{Enhanced} = I(x,y) - w \cdot \nabla^2 I(x,y)$, considering $w = 1$.

The effect of improving the sharpness of an image can be carried out in a single execution. Considering $w = 1$, the model of enhancement can be defined as follows:

$$I(x,y)_{En} = I(x,y) - (1) \cdot \nabla^2 I(x,y) \tag{3.29}$$

If it is replaced by the Laplacian from Equation 3.29 with the expression of Equation 3.27, the enhancement model is modeled as follows:

$$I(x,y)_{En} = 5I(x,y) - \left[I(x+1,y) + I(x-1,y) \right.$$
$$\left. + I(x,y+1) + I(x,y-1) \right] \tag{3.30}$$

If Equation 3.30 is presented in the form of a filter, the coefficient matrix is defined as follows:

$$I(x,y)_{Enhanced} = \begin{bmatrix} 0 & -1 & 0 \\ -1 & 5 & -1 \\ 0 & -1 & 0 \end{bmatrix} \tag{3.31}$$

Figure 3.16 presents the result of applying this filter to an image.

3.4.3 Use of MATLAB for the Implementation of the Laplacian Filter and the Enhancement of Sharpness

In this section, the use of MATLAB to improve the sharpness of images is described. In this process, it is also necessary to calculate the Laplacian. The MATLAB code to improve the sharpness of an image can be divided into two simple steps. In the first step, the Laplacian filter is calculated from the filter described in Figure 3.12. In the second step, the image sharpness is generated considering the information of low frequency contained in the original image minus the value of the Laplacian (see Equation 3.28), which incorporates the information that allows the enhancement of the details of the image. Program 3.2 shows the coding in MATLAB to improve the sharpness of an image using the Laplacian.

PROGRAM 3.2. IMPROVING THE SHARPNESS OF AN IMAGE THROUGH THE APPLICATION OF THE LAPLACIAN OPERATOR WITH MATLAB

```
%%%%%%%%%%%%%%%%%%%%%%%%%%%%%%%%%%%%%%%%%%%%%%%%%%%%%%%%%%%%%%%%%%%%%%
%%%%%%%%%%%%%
% Improving the sharpness of an image using the Laplacian
operator %
%%%%%%%%%%%%%%%%%%%%%%%%%%%%%%%%%%%%%%%%%%%%%%%%%%%%%%%%%%%%%%%%%%%%%%
%%%%%%%%%%%%%
%SThe image is read in order to process it.
I=imread('img.jpg');
% A conversion is made in the color space to work with
% an intensity image
Im=rgb2gray(I);
% The factor with which the Laplacian operator
% affect the image (see Equation 3.32)
w=1;
% The dimension values of the image are obtained:
[m,n]=size(Im);
% The image is converted to double to avoid problems in
the conversion of the data type:
Im=double(Im);
% The matrix L is created with zeros:
L=zeros(size(Im));

% FIRST PART.
% The Laplacian filter is applied:
for x=2:m-1
    for y=2:n-1
        L(x,y)= m(x+1,y)+Im(x-1,y)+Im(x,y+1)+Im(x,y-1)-
4*Im(x,y);
    end
end
% SECOND PART.
% The new pixels of the image whose sharpness
% is intended to improve (see Formula 3.32):
Init=Im-w*L;
% The minimum value for the Init image is obtained:
VminInit=min(min(Init));
% Using the minimum value shifts to avoid negatives:
```

```
GradOffL=Init-VminInit;
% The maximum value to normalize to 1 is obtained:
VmaxInit=max(max(GradOffL));
% The gradients are normalized to 255:
InitN=(GradOffL/VmaxInit)*255;
% Convert the image for deployment:
GInitN=uint8(InitN);
% The image is displayed to analyze its results
figure
imshow(GInitN)
```

The results of applying the code presented in Program 3.2 are shown in Figure 3.17. In this figure, it can be seen the difference between the original grayscale image and the image with contrast enhancement for $w = 1$.

3.4.4 The Canny Filter

A well-known method for detecting edges in images is the Canny filter [2]. This method is based on the application of a series of filters in different directions and resolutions, which are finally combined into a single result. The method aims to achieve three different objectives: (a) to minimize the number of false edges, (b) to improve the location of edges in the image, and (c) to deliver an image whose edge width is only one pixel. The Canny filter is essentially a filter based on gradient methods, but, however, it also uses the second derivative, or Laplacian, as a criterion for edge location. Most of the time, this algorithm is used in its simple form, that is, setting only the smoothing parameter σ. Figure 3.18 shows examples of the application of this algorithm using different values of the parameter σ.

(a)

(b)

FIGURE 3.17
Results of applying the code of Program 3.2 to improve the sharpness of an image through the application of the Laplacian operator with MATLAB®, (a) original grayscale image, and (b) image with improved contrast for $w = 1$.

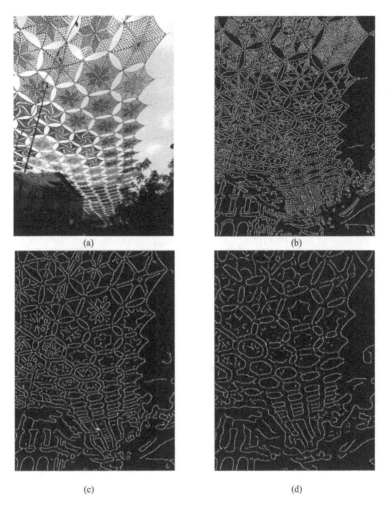

FIGURE 3.18

Canny's algorithm applied to an image. (a) Original image, (b) image edges with $\sigma = 2$, (c) image edges with $\sigma = 4$, and (d) image edges with $\sigma = 6$.

3.4.5 MATLAB Tools that Implement the Canny Filter

Due to the wide use of the Canny filter as a previous stage in the segmentation and classification of objects and its robustness in determining edges, the filter is normally implemented in most commercial libraries and digital image processing tools. In MATLAB, the Canny algorithm can be calculated using the edge function. Its general structure is described as follows:

```
BW = edge(I, 'canny', U, sigma);
```

where BW is the image with the edges extracted, considering the Canny algorithm. I is the grayscale image from which the edges will be extracted. U is the threshold value from which the pixels are classified as edges. sigma represents the smoothing parameter (σ) that has the effect of minimizing the number of false edges.

References

[1] Gose, E., Johnsonbaugh, R., & Jost, S. (2017). *Pattern recognition and image analysis.* CRC Press.

[2] Canny, J. (1986). A computational approach to edge detection. *IEEE Transactions on Pattern Analysis and Machine Intelligence,* 8(6), 679–698. https://ieeexplore.ieee.org/document/4767851

[3] Bina, S., & Ghassemian, H. (2019). A Comprehensive Review of Edge Detection Techniques for Images in Computer Vision. *Journal of Computer and Communications,* 7(1), 36–49. https://doi.org/10.14257/ijmue.2017.12.11.01

[4] Hussain, S., & Hussain, M. (2014). A Review of Edge Detection Techniques in Digital Image Processing. *International Journal of Scientific and Engineering Research,* 5(2), 222–231. https://www.researchgate.net/journal/International-Journal-of-Science-and-Research-IJSR-2319-7064

[5] Singh, S., & Bhatnagar, G. (2015). Comparative Analysis of Edge Detection Techniques for Digital Images. *Journal of Information Technology and Computer Science,* 7(1), 31–40. https://doi.org/10.1109/ICCCIS51004.2021.9397225

[6] Abdullah-Al-Wadud, M., Islam, M. A., & Islam, M. M. (2017). A Review of Image Edge Detection Techniques and Algorithms. *Journal of Electromagnetic Analysis and Applications,* 9(10), 240–251.https://doi.org/10.1007/s11633-018-1117-z

[7] Solomon, C., & Breckon, T. (2010). *Fundamentals of Digital Image Processing: A Practical Approach with Examples in MATLAB.* Wiley.

[8] Tariq, M. A., Raza, A., & Abbas, M. (2019). A Comparative Study of Edge Detection Techniques in Digital Image Processing. *IEEE Access,* 7, 40793–40807. https://doi.org/10.46565/jreas.2021.v06i04.001

4

Segmentation and Processing
of Binary Images

4.1 Introduction

Image segmentation is considered an active field of research in the area of computer vision with an innumerable number of applications [1]. The purpose of segmentation is to divide an image into regions that, according to some context, have some relationship or meaning. Various methods and approaches have been proposed in the literature for this purpose. The choice of a particular method depends on the characteristics of the application. The segmentation must be considered as a previous step for the description, recognition, or classification of objects contained in an image [2]. This chapter will analyze the most popular segmentation methods and their implementation.

The binary images produced as a result of the segmentation process are images whose pixels only have one value out of two possible ones, or zero [3]. Normally, this pixel classification corresponds to the object (values set to one) and the background (values set to zero), although obviously, such differentiation in real images is not always possible. In this chapter, the structure of binary images will also be analyzed, considering how to isolate each of the objects present in the image and how to describe them structurally. As a simple definition, an object will be defined as a group of pixels that are connected by some kind of neighborhood while its surroundings are bordered by pixels of value zero (the background).

4.2 Segmentation

Segmentation is defined as the process of dividing the image into different regions so that the pixels in each region are similar (according to certain criteria) while they are different between the regions [4]. The objective is to distinguish between objects of interest and the rest of the image. In the simplest

DOI: 10.1201/9781003287414-4

case, the segmentation is conducted by considering only two classes. The first class considers the object of interest, while the second class corresponds to the rest of the image, commonly known as the background. This process is also called binarization [5].

The most commonly used criterion in segmentation is the homogeneity of grayscale regions, although for more advanced applications, color or texture can also be used. Segmentation is often the first step in a pattern recognition system. Its function is to isolate the objects of interest for later classification [6].

There are many approaches to image segmentation, which can be divided according to the characteristics considered and the type of algorithm used. According to the characteristics, the segmentation methods include the intensity values of the pixels, the texture, or the magnitude of the gradient. Regarding the type of algorithm, segmentation techniques can be divided into contextual and non-contextual [7].

Non-contextual techniques ignore the relationship between pixels and the object they are trying to isolate. In this way, the pixels are grouped considering some global characteristics of them, such as intensity level. Among the main techniques of this category is thresholding. In thresholding, each pixel is assigned to a particular category based on its intensity level, depending on whether it exceeds a predetermined level known as a threshold.

Contextual techniques, different from non-contextual methods, additionally exploit the relationship between the pixel and the object to be isolated by incorporating homogeneity measures or criteria. In this way, a contextual method could group a set of pixels that have similar intensity and that, at the same time, are close to each other or that maintain the same direction according to their gradient value.

4.3 Threshold

Thresholding is a segmentation technique that assumes that objects are integrated by pixels of homogeneous intensity. In this way, each pixel is compared with a pre-fixed threshold; if the pixel intensity value is higher, the pixel is considered to belong to a certain category, but if it is lower, it will correspond to another category. Under these circumstances, the quality of the segmentation will depend on the choice of the appropriate threshold value [8].

In the ideal case of thresholding, the histogram that reflects the pixel distribution of the objects present in the image does not overlap, so a certain threshold value can divide both objects. Figure 4.1a shows an image containing two different square objects: A and B. Object A involves pixels with an intensity from a Gaussian distribution with a mean of 60 and a standard

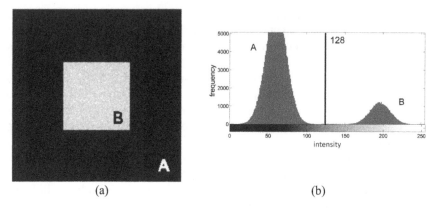

(a)   (b)

FIGURE 4.1
Distribution of the intensities of the pixels that integrate two different objects in an image.
(a) The two objects and (b) their distribution in the histogram.

deviation of 10. Object B has pixels from a Gaussian distribution with a mean of 190 and a standard deviation of 10. Figure 4.1b shows the corresponding histogram of image 4.1a.

From Figure 4.1, both objects can be clearly segmented if a threshold of 128 is applied. Therefore, if the intensity of a certain pixel is greater than 128, this pixel belongs to object B. Otherwise, it is considered to belong to object A. Figure 4.2 shows the result of this binarization.

In most cases, the distribution of the pixels does not maintain a division as clear as the one shown in Figure 4.1. On the contrary, the distributions tend to have overlapping regions. Indeed, the magnitude of this overlapping determines the difficulty of the segmentation since the greater the extent, the more difficult it is to determine which pixels belong to one or another distribution. Figure 4.3 shows an example of this case.

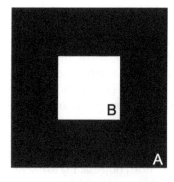

FIGURE 4.2
The result of the segmentation of Figure 4.1(a) considering the value of 128 as the threshold.

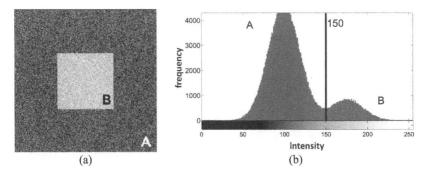

(a)   (b)

FIGURE 4.3
Objects that overlap their distributions. (a) The two objects and (b) their distribution in the histogram.

In cases of overlapping in the distributions, it is not possible to find a threshold that satisfies a correct segmentation since the belonging of the pixels in the overlap is not clear. To illustrate such an effect on segmentation, the image presented in Figure 4.3 is binarized, considering the threshold of 150, which approximately represents a division between the two modes produced by the distributions. The result of the binarization is shown in Figure 4.4. In the result, several pixels can be seen that could not be properly classified due to the existing overlap between the distributions of both objects.

The uncertainty caused by the overlapping of the distributions represents the cause of the poor results in the segmentation. An auxiliary technique for eliminating the overlap between distributions is the application of the median filter to the original image as a pre-processing method. Figure 4.5 shows the image that results from the application of the median filter (applied in image 4.3a) and the separation effect on its final histogram. In the processing, a 3×3 neighborhood was used.

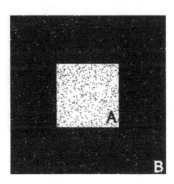

FIGURE 4.4
The result of the segmentation of Figure 4.3(a) considering the value of 128 as the threshold.

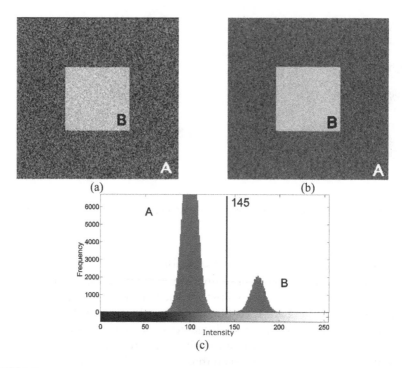

FIGURE 4.5

Effect of using the median filter on overlapped distributions. (a) The original image, (b) the image obtained by the median filter, and (c) the resulting distribution.

As a result of the application of the median filter, the overlapping of the distributions is eliminated in such a way that, by choosing an appropriate threshold, a perfect binarization of the image is obtained. Figure 4.6 shows the result of the binarization.

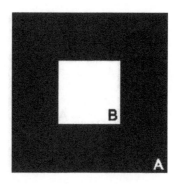

FIGURE 4.6

Result of the segmentation of Figure 4.b (a) considering the value of 145 as the threshold.

4.4 The Optimal Threshold

The use of the median filter does not always allow the elimination of the overlapping between two densities present in the histogram. In such circumstances, the optimal threshold must be calculated, which produces the least number of misclassified pixels. This is the set of pixels belonging to object A that are classified as if they belonged to object B and vice versa. In this way, the optimal threshold corresponds to the intercept between both distributions. Figure 4.7 graphically shows the optimal threshold for a hypothetical example of distribution. The figure shows the distributions of two objects A and B that present an overlapping region T. From the figure; the intersection point clearly represents the best location to define the classification limit for each of the classes represented by their respective distributions.

There are several approaches for determining the optimal threshold in the case of the overlapping of two distributions. Most of them operate iteratively, testing a certain threshold in such a way that the pixels of each object are closer to the average value of their respective intensities than to the average intensity value of the opposite object.

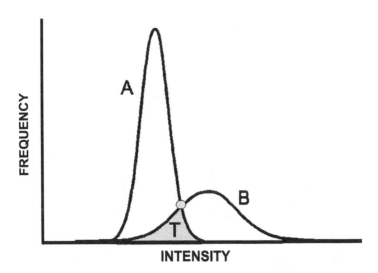

FIGURE 4.7
The optimal threshold for the binarization of two objects according to the overlapping of their distributions.

4.5 Otsu Algorithm

The Otsu method is the most popular method for calculating the optimal threshold. The method allows the binarization of two classes using the histogram of image intensities. The method considers an image I of dimension $M \times N$ with $L-1$ gray scales. The histogram presents two overlapping areas from the distribution. The first corresponds to object A, which involves the intensity values from 0 to k, while the second integrates the gray levels from $k+1$ to $L-1$. Figure 4.8 illustrates the distribution and its associated variables.

The Otsu method starts by calculating the probabilities of each object or class:

$$P(A) = \sum_{i=0}^{k} h(i) = w_A(k) = w(k)$$

$$P(B) = \sum_{i=k+1}^{L-1} h(i) = w_B(k) = 1 - w(k)$$

(4.1)

where $h(i)$ represents the number of pixels of intensity i contained in the image. Under these conditions, the average intensity of each object can be calculated as follows:

$$\mu_A(k) = \frac{1}{w_A(k)} \sum_{i=0}^{k} i \cdot h(i)$$

$$\mu_B(k) = \frac{1}{w_B(k)} \sum_{i=k+1}^{L-1} i \cdot h(i)$$

(4.2)

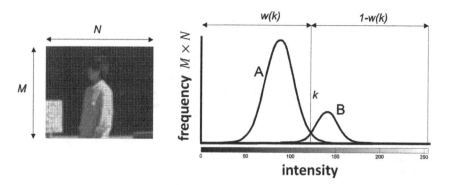

FIGURE 4.8
Segmentation process of two distributions using the Otsu method.

From these values, the variances can be obtained as follows:

$$\sigma_A^2(k) = \frac{1}{w_A(k)} \sum_{i=0}^{k} \left(i - \mu_A(k) \right)^2 \cdot h(i)$$

$$\sigma_B^2(k) = \frac{1}{w_B(k)} \sum_{i=k+1}^{L-1} \left(i - \mu_B(k) \right)^2 \cdot h(i)$$

(4.3)

Under these circumstances, the variance within classes can be defined in terms of their variances according to the following expression:

$$\sigma_D^2 = w_A(k) \cdot \sigma_A^2(k) + w_B(k) \cdot \sigma_B^2(k) \tag{4.4}$$

Considering this formulation, the Otsu method searches for the optimal threshold that represents the intensity level k, which minimizes the variance within the classes (Equation 4.4). Therefore, the objective is to determine the variance value of each object so small that it can minimize their overlap. With the models defined so far, an algorithm could attempt all the possible values of k and return the element for which the value of σ_D^2 is minimum. However, it is possible to develop a recursive formulation that implies faster computation. This requires calculating several terms, such as the total variance and the variance between objects or classes.

The total variance of the distribution calculates the variance of the entire histogram. Thus, its calculation is defined as follows:

$$\sigma_T^2 = \sum_{i=0}^{L-1} \left(i - \mu_T \right)^2 \cdot h(i) \tag{4.5}$$

where μ_T represents the average intensity of the histogram that represents the distribution:

$$\mu_T = \sum_{i=0}^{L-1} i \cdot h(i) \tag{4.6}$$

Finally, the variance between classes σ_E^2 can be considered as the subtraction between the total variance σ_T^2 and the variance within the classes or objects σ_T^2. Therefore, σ_E^2 is defined by the following expression:

$$\sigma_E^2 = \sigma_T^2 - \sigma_D^2$$

$$= w(k) \cdot \left(\mu_A(k) - \mu_T \right)^2 - \left(1 - w(k) \right) \cdot \left(\mu_B(k) - \mu_T \right) \tag{4.7}$$

$$= w(k) \cdot \left(1 - w(k) \right) \cdot \left(\mu_A(k) - \mu_B(k) \right)^2$$

Since the total variance is always constant and independent of the intensity level k, the effect of calculating the optimal threshold depends on only the variances σ_E^2 and σ_D^2. Therefore, minimizing the variance within the classes σ_D^2 is equivalent to maximizing the variance between the classes σ_E^2. The advantage of maximizing σ_E^2 is that it can be computed recursively as the values of k are iterated. Under such conditions, the equations for this recursion are defined below, considering that their initial values are $w(1) = h(1)$ and $\mu_A(0) = 0$.

$$w(k+1) = w(k) + h(k+1)$$

$$\mu_A(k+1) = \frac{\left(w(k) \cdot \mu_A(k) + (k+1) \cdot h(k+1)\right)}{w(k+1)} \tag{4.8}$$

$$\mu_B(k+1) = \frac{\left(\mu_T - w(k+1) \cdot \mu_A(k+1)\right)}{1 - w(k+1)}$$

By using these expressions, it is possible to update σ_E^2 and test if its value is the maximum as the intensity level k increases progressively. This simple optimization method can be used without problems because the function σ_E^2 is always smooth and unimodal. Program 4.1 shows the implementation of the Otsu method. In the program, a color image is first transformed into a grayscale image. Then the Otsu method is implemented according to the steps shown in Equations 4.1–4.8. Figure 4.9 shows the original image and the binarization result obtained by Program 4.1.

PROGRAM 4.1.   IMPLEMENTATION OF THE OTSU METHOD FOR THE BINARIZATION OF DISTRIBUTION OF TWO OVERLAPPING CLASSES

```
%%%%%%%%%%%%%%%%%%%%%%%%%%%%%%%%%%%%%%%%%%%%%%%%%%%%%%%%%%%%%%%%%%%%%%
%%%%%%%%%%%%
% Function to calculate the optimal threshold Otsu method
%%%%%%%%%%%%%%%%%%%%%%%%%%%%%%%%%%%%%%%%%%%%%%%%%%%%%%%%%%%%%%%%%%%%%%
%%%%%%%%%%%%

function ImF = otsu(ImI)
% Convert RGB image to grayscale
IG=rgb2gray(ImI);
% Histogram is calculated
histogramCounts=imhist(IG);
% Total pixels in the image
total = sum(histogramCounts);
% Accumulation of variables is initialized
sumA = 0;
```

```
wA = 0;
maximum = 0.0;
% The total average of the histogram is calculated
sum1 = dot( (0:255), histogramCounts);
% Each intensity level k is tested
for k=1:256
    % Equation 4.1 P(A)
    wA = wA + histogramCounts(k);
    if (wA == 0)
        continue;
    end
    % Equation 4.2 P(B)
    wB = total - wA;
    if (wB == 0)
        break;
    end
    % Average is calculated for class A
    sumA = sumA + (k-1) * histogramCounts(k);
    mA = sumA / wA;
    % Average is calculated for class B
    mB = (sum1 - sumA) / wB;
    % The variance between classes is calculated Equation
4.7
    VE = wA * wB * (mA - mB) * (mA - mB);
    % It is tested if the maximum has been found
    % If it is found, it is saved in threshold
    if ( VE >= maximum )
        threshold = k;
        maximum = VE;
    end
end
ImF=IG>=threshold;
end
```

4.6 Segmentation by Region Growth

The region growth method is a segmentation algorithm based on the successive integration of pixels that are related according to a similarity criterion.

Using this approach, a pixel in the image must be chosen as the starting point. Then, its neighboring pixels are analyzed to check if any of them are similar to it. If it is similar, the pixel is included as part of the segmented region. Otherwise, it will not be considered.

Thus, the first step in the region growth method is to select an initial pixel or seed pixel s(x,y). Its selection is important since it must be contained in the region in which it is intended to segment. From the selection of this pixel,

(a)

(b)

FIGURE 4.9
Results of the Otsu method for binarization produced by Program 4.1. (a) Original image and (b) result image.

a local search is made around $s(x,y)$ to find a pixel with similar characteristics. The similarity criteria are very diverse, and these could include texture, color, etc. The most common is intensity. Therefore, if the neighboring pixel is similar, it is included as part of the segmented region; otherwise, it is registered in a list L to subsequently consider such elements in the search for other pixels. Next, the region growth algorithm will be described step by step in order to describe the complete computational process.

4.6.1 Initial Pixel

The initial pixel or seed pixel $s(x,y)$ must be chosen in such a way that it is within the region on which it is desired to segment. However, if additional information is considered, such as its position, this situation could speed up the segmentation process. An easy way to select it is through an interactive method. Under this approach, the point is selected directly from the image. For this purpose, MATLAB® implements the function getpts. This function has the following format:

`[y,x]=getpts();`

where x and y represent the coordinates selected interactively with the mouse; notice how the coordinates are inverted. This is because the information is delivered in a matrix, first the row (coordinate y) and then the column (coordinate x). It is important before using the getpts function to display the image using imshow. In this way, the current graphics identifier, as provided by imshow, can be utilized by getpts. Another issue of importance represents the fact that the getpts function returns the values of the coordinates of the graphic object provided by the image displayed using imshow. For this reason, values are frequently obtained with decimal numbers, which are not appropriate to serve as indices in the selection of a matrix element. Therefore, it is necessary to truncate or cast the content of the variable to an integer type.

4.6.2 Local Search

Once the initial pixel s(x,y) is selected, the method performs a local search around it, checking similar pixels recursively. Therefore, the search process is carried out in neighborhood **V** around the four closest neighbors. Once a pixel has been found within the neighborhood with similar characteristics to the initial pixel, it replaces the role of the seed pixel, and the local search process is repeated.

The best way to implement a 4-element search neighborhood is to define an array of the form $\mathbf{V}=[-1\ 0; 1\ 0; 0\ -1; 0\ 1]$. Each line expresses a particular neighbor element, while the columns indicate the displacements in the direction of horizontal (Δx) and vertical (Δy). Figure 4.10 illustrates the correspondence process between Matrix **V** and the neighborhood.

Within the search process, two important problems arise: pixels outside the image field and the search direction. The first problem occurs mainly

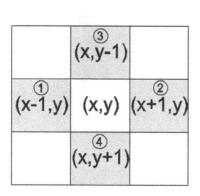
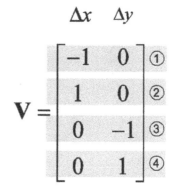

FIGURE 4.10
Correspondence process between Matrix **V** and the neighborhood.

when the search is carried out within the limits of the image, and due to the displacements, the selected pixel does not exist within the image. This situation is solved by adding a condition to the code that allows evaluating if the selected pixel exists within the limits defined for the image.

The second problem appears when, in the local search, the displacement of the pixels takes a certain direction; however, in the opposite direction, there are pixels that, according to the similarity measure, correspond to the region to be seeded. Under these conditions, the search process should be able to modify the direction when searching in a determined direction has already been exhausted. To solve this, a list L is implemented to store the unselected pixels. The position of the pixel and its intensity are recorded in the list. Therefore, the list is used in the comparison. So, when a new pixel **pn** has been found locally, its intensity is compared with the elements contained in the list L. From this comparison, it could happen that a distant pixel **pd** is similar to **pn**, which would imply that pixels with similar characteristics have already been exhausted in the vicinity of **pn**. Under such conditions, a change of direction is necessary. Each time a pixel with similar characteristics is found within the local search process, the information of this pixel is extracted from the list. This action determines that the pixel information is already part of the segmented region **R**. Figure 4.11 shows the store process of the list L for an image. In the image, it can be seen how the search that begins in the seed pixel **s(x,y)** has followed the direction marked by the

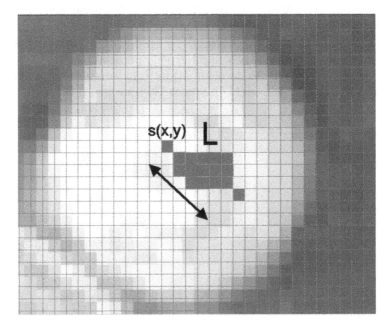

FIGURE 4.11
Store process of list L for an image.

arrow, when pixels with the characteristics to be segmented are also found in opposite directions.

In order to check if a pixel is similar to another, considering the intensity as a similarity criterion (as is the common case), two parameters are important for the region-growing segmentation method: (A) the maximum permissible dissimilarity and (B) the similarity of the segmented region.

The maximum permissible dissimilarity (**Mp**) represents the maximum possible difference between two pixels that is considered similar. This element is considered a configuration parameter. Therefore, the searching process will be executed until the difference between the members of the list **L** and the new pixel **pn** is higher than **Mp**.

The segmented region similarity (**Srs**) defines the average intensity of the region to be segmented. This parameter allows for more robust segmentations since its value is iteratively updated each time a new pixel is found within the segmented region R. The **Srs** parameter is calculated considering the following model:

$$\mathbf{Srs}(k+1) = \frac{\mathbf{Srs}(k) \cdot |R| + I(pn)}{|R| + 1} \tag{4.9}$$

where the value of $\mathbf{Srs}(k+1)$ represents the updated value of $\mathbf{Srs}(k)$, while $|R|$ corresponds to the number of elements currently part of the segmented region. Finally, $I(pn)$ defines the intensity of the new pixel **pn**.

Program 4.2 shows the MATLAB code that implements the region-growing segmentation method. Figure 4.12 exhibits the original image and the image obtained as a result of the operation of Program 4.2.

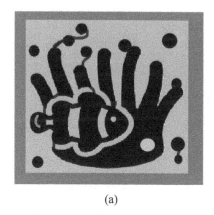
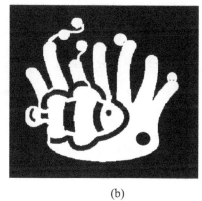

(a) (b)

FIGURE 4.12

Results of the region growing segmentation method produced by Program 4.2. (a) Original image and (b) the resulting image.

PROGRAM 4.2. IMPLEMENTATION OF THE REGION GROWTH SEGMENTATION METHOD

```
%%%%%%%%%%%%%%%%%%%%%%%%%%%%%%%%%%%%%%%%
% Region-growing Segmentation Method
%%%%%%%%%%%%%%%%%%%%%%%%%%%%%%%%%%%%%%%%

% Clear all memory
clear all
% Store the image in the variable I1
I1=imread('fotos/bill.jpg');
% Converts to the grayscale
IG=rgb2gray(I1);
% Converts to data type double
I=im2double(IG);
% The image is displayed
imshow(I);
% The initial pixel or seed ps is obtained
[y,x]=getpts();
% The maximum permissible dissimilarity is defined
Mp=0.25;
% The values obtained from the coordinates are truncated
x=floor(x);
y=floor(y);
% the final image
J = zeros(size(I));
Isizes = size(I); % Dimensions are obtained
% Initial value of the similarity of the segmented region
Srs = I(x,y);
R = 1; % Number of pixels in the region
% Memory is reserved for operation
neg_free = 10000; neg_pos=0;
L = zeros(neg_free,3); % List length
% Initial similarity
pixdist=0;
% Neighbors for local search
V=[-1 0; 1 0; 0 -1;0 1];
% Start the process of the method
while(pixdist<Mp&&R<numel(I))
    % Local search
    for j=1:4
        % Calculate the new position
        xn = x +V(j,1); yn = y +V(j,2);
      % It checks if the pixel is inside the image
  ins=(xn>=1)&&(yn>=1)&&(xn<=Isizes(1))&&(yn<=Isizes(2));
        % It checks if the pixel is already in the list L
        if(ins&&(J(xn,yn)==0))
                neg_pos = neg_pos+1;
```

```
                    L(neg_pos,:) = [xn yn I(xn,yn)]; J(xn,yn)=1;
         end
      end

      % If more memory is needed, add
      if (neg_pos+10>neg_free), neg_free=neg_free+10000;
L((neg_pos+1):neg_free,:)=0;
      end
      % The similarity of the pixel with the list is
checked
      dist = abs(L(1:neg_pos,3)-Srs);
      [pixdist, index] = min(dist);
      J(x,y)=2; R=R+1;

      % Calculate the new similarity of the segmented
region
      Srs= (Srs*R + L(index,3))/(R+1);

      % The found pixel is the new pixel
      x = L(index,1); y = L(index,2);

      % Your features are removed from the list
      L(index,:)=L(neg_pos,:); neg_pos=neg_pos-1;
   end
   % It is recorded as part of the segmented region R
   J=J>1;
   figure
   imshow(J)
```

4.7 Labeling of Objects in Binary Images

Object labeling is a classic image processing technique that is known in the literature and vision community as "region labeling". A binary image is a numerical representation that presents only two classes of elements: ones (that indicate a specific object) and zeros (that correspond to the background). An example of a digital image with different objects is shown in Figure 4.13. Under region labeling, the objective is to identify the number of binary objects contained in an image. The algorithm essentially consists of two steps: (1) temporary labeling of the objects and (2) the solution of multiple pixel labels belonging to the same object. The method is relatively complex (especially step 2). However, due to its moderate memory requirements, it represents a good choice for object labeling. The complete algorithm is described in Algorithm 4.1.

FIGURE 4.13
Binary image with four elements.

4.7.1 Temporary Labeling of Objects (Step 1)

In the first step, the image is analyzed from left to right and from top to bottom. At each movement, each pixel (x,y) is assigned a temporary label. The value of the label depends on the type of neighborhood defined, which can be 4-neighbors or 8-neighbors. For each case, the used mask can be defined as follows:

$$
N_4(x,y) = \begin{bmatrix} \cdot & N_2 & \cdot \\ N_1 & \times & \cdot \\ \cdot & \cdot & \cdot \end{bmatrix} \quad N_8(x,y) = \begin{bmatrix} N_2 & N_3 & N_4 \\ N_1 & \times & \cdot \\ \cdot & \cdot & \cdot \end{bmatrix} \quad (4.10)
$$

where $\times$ identifies the current pixel at position (x,y). In the case of 4-neighbors, only the pixels $N_1 = I(x-1,y)$ and $N_2 = I(x,y-1)$ are considered, while in the case of 8-neighbors, the pixels $N_1,\ldots,N_4$ are considered. Figure 4.14 shows the complete process of step 1 carried out on an image and considers the 8-neighbor neighborhood as the criterion.

ALGORITHM 4.1.   LABELING ALGORITHM

Object labeling ($I_b(x,y)$)

$I_b(x,y)$ Binary image 1 $\rightarrow$ object and 0 $\rightarrow$ background.

Of dimensions $M \times N$

1: <u>Step 1.</u> Initial labels are assigned.

2: $m = 2$ is initialized as the next label to assign.

3: An empty set C is created to record the collisions.

4: **for** $y = 1,...,M$ **do**

4: **for** $x = 1,...,N$ **do**

if $\left(I(x,y) = 1\right)$ **then**

6:

7: **if** (all neighboring pixels are $=0$) **then**

8: $I(x,y) = m$

9: $m = m + 1$

10: **else if** exactly one neighboring pixel already has a label n_k **then**

11: $I(x,y) = n_k$

12: **else if** several neighboring pixels already have some labels n_j **then**

13: Select some label such that

$I(x,y) = k, \quad k \in n_j$

14: for all other neighbors with labels $n_i > 1$ and $n_i \neq k$ do

15: Record the collision pair n_i, k in the set C, such that

$C = C \bigcup \{n_i, k\}$

16: <u>Step 2.</u> Collisions are resolved

17: Let $E = \{2, 3, ..., m\}$ be the set of preliminarily assigned labels.

18: A partition of E is performed, represented by a vector of sets, one set for each label: $R = [R_2, R_3..., R_m]$ so, $R = [R_2, R_3..., R_m]$ *for all* $i \in E$.

19: **for** all collisions $a, b \in C$ **do**

20: The sets R_a and R_b containing the labels a and b are found in R.

$R_a \rightarrow$ The set that currently contains the label a.

21: $R_b \rightarrow$ The set that currently contains the label b.

22:   **if** $R_a \neq R_b$ **then**

Join the sets R_a and R_b, such that:

$$R_a = R_a \bigcup R_b$$

23: $R_b = \{\ \}$

24:   <u>Step 3.</u> Re-labeling of the image

25:   It traverses all the pixels of the image

26:   **if** $I(x,y) > 1$ **then**

27:   Find the set R_i in R which contains the label $I(x,y)$

A unique and representative element k is chosen from the set R_i (for example the minimum value).

28:   The label is replaced at the current pixel, $I(x,y) = k$.

29:   The value of $I(x,y)$ already labeled is returned.

4.7.2 Propagation of Labeling

It is considered that the pixel value of the object in a given position is $I(x,y) = 1$, while for a given background position, it is $I(x,y) = 0$. In addition, it is also assumed that the pixels outside the image are zero or part of the background. The neighborhood region is considered horizontally first and then vertically, defining the upper left corner as the starting point. In the process, if the current pixel $I(x,y)$ is one, then a new label is assigned to it, or an existing one is assigned to it of one of its neighbors $N(x,y)$ already has one. Therefore, the choice of the type of neighborhood (4-neighbors or 8-neighbors) for the determination of labels has a great impact on the final result. Figure 4.14 exhibits the process of propagation of labeling.

4.7.3 Adjacent Tagging

If two or more neighbors contain different labels, then a label collision occurs; that is, pixels that are grouped together to form the same object have a different label. For example, an object with the shape of a "U" will have different labels assigned to the left and right sides; this is because, during the

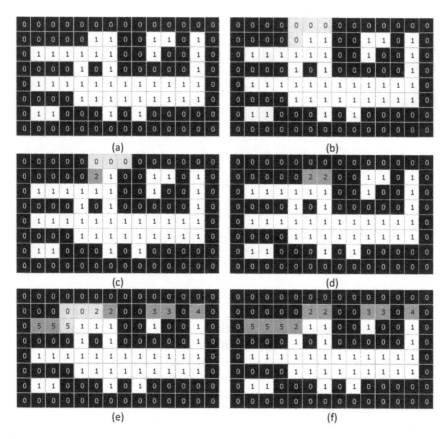

FIGURE 4.14
Propagation of the labeling process. (a) Original image. The first pixel in one is found in (b), all its neighboring pixels are zero. Therefore, the pixel receives the label of 2 (c). At the next iteration (d), a neighboring pixel has a label of 2, so the current pixel assumes this value as its label. In (e), there are two neighboring pixels with the labels 2 and 5, one of these values will be assumed by the current pixel, and the collision that occurred should be registered 2, 5.

displacement of the mask along the image, it is not possible to identify that the object is connected in the down part.

When two different labels are present on the same object (as in the previous case), a label collision occurs. This collision is not processed directly in step 1 but is only recorded for further processing in step 2. The number of collisions present depends on the content of the image and can only be known after step 1 has been completed.

As a result of the first step, we have an image with the pixels temporarily labeled, as well as a list of detected collisions among pixels belonging to the same object. Figure 4.15a shows the result of an image after step 1; all the pixels have a temporary label, while the collisions are registered and marked by

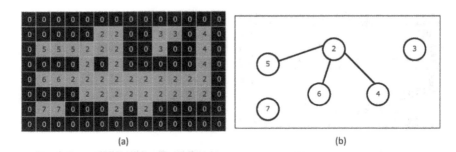

(a)   (b)

FIGURE 4.15
Result of step 1 in the labeling process. Label collisions are represented by circles (a), labels and (b) collisions corresponding to nodes of a graph.

circles in the correspondence 2, 4, 2, 5 and 2, 6. With this, we have the labels $E = \{2,3,4,5,6,7\}$ and the collisions $C = \{2,4,2,5,2,6\}$, which correspond to the nodes of an undirected graph shown in Figure 4.15b.

4.7.4 Collision Resolution (Step 2)

The task of the second pass is to solve the collisions recorded in the first pass. This process is not easy since two different labels, tentatively belonging to two different objects, may be connected through a third object. This task is identical to the problem of finding connected components of a graph, where the labels E calculated in step 1 represent the nodes of the graph, while the collisions C their connections (Figure 4.15).

After counting the different labels belonging to the same object, the value of the label of each pixel of that object is replaced by a general label corresponding to the smallest of those within it (see Figure 4.16).

0	0	0	0	0	0	0	0	0	0	0	0	0	0
0	0	0	0	0	2	2	0	0	3	3	0	2	0
0	2	2	2	2	2	2	0	0	3	0	0	2	0
0	0	0	0	2	0	2	0	0	0	0	0	2	0
0	2	2	2	2	2	2	2	2	2	2	2	2	0
0	0	0	0	2	2	2	2	2	2	2	2	2	0
0	7	7	0	0	0	2	0	2	0	0	0	0	0
0	0	0	0	0	0	0	0	0	0	0	0	0	0

FIGURE 4.16
Result of the object labeling process after the second step. All temporarily assigned labels are replaced by the smallest numerical label contained in the object

In this section, the algorithm to identify the number of objects present in a binary image through its labeling has been described. The idea after having performed this algorithm is to have a label for each object contained in the image in such a way that it can be easily identified.

4.7.5 Implementation of the Object Labeling Algorithm Using MATLAB

This section explains how to implement the object labeling program described in Algorithm 4.1. Program 4.1 implements in MATLAB each of the three steps in which the algorithm has been divided. In the first step, the image is processed from right to left and from top to bottom. In general, during this process, a temporal label is assigned to each pixel of the image depending on whether it does not have labeled neighbors or has one or more. In the second step, the registered collisions are solved by considering the pixels that belong to the regions that have a neighborhood conflict. This process is implemented through two nested *for's* that allow the label exchange for each of the elements in the image. The for loop used for the label exchange is determined by the label number whose value is the minimum (compared to the other in question). In the third step, the labels are reassigned. In this third step, several labels are eliminated due to the solution of collisions. Once the absolute number of labels is obtained, it would be very simple to use a for loop to reassign the labels so that they appear continuously. To implement this process, the unique function is used. The unique function obtains the sequence of unique values contained in an array; by unique, it means that no matter how many times this value is repeated in the array, it will only be presented once by the unique function. Its general syntax is:

```
b = unique(A)
```

where A is a matrix whose unique values contained in it are explored, while b is a vector that contains the values contained in the matrix without repetition; therefore, the value of b applied to our implementation will contain the labels that remained after performing the collision resolution process.

PROGRAM 4.3. PROGRAM TO LABEL OBJECTS IN A BINARY IMAGE. THE PROGRAM IMPLEMENTS THE ALGORITHM DESCRIBED IN ALGORITHM 4.1

```
%%%%%%%%%%%%%%%%%%%%%%%%%%%%%%%%%%%%%%%%%%%%%%%%%%%%%%%
% Program to label the objects in a Binary image
%%%%%%%%%%%%%%%%%%%%%%%%%%%%%%%%%%%%%%%%%%%%%%%%%%%%%%%
clear all
close all
I=imread('fotos/figuras.jpg');
```

```
I=rgb2gray(I);
Ib=imbinarize(I);
Ib=1-Ib;
figure; imshow(Ib);
% The dimensions of the binary image are obtained
% where 0 is the background and 1 the objects
[m n]=size(Ib);
% The binary image is converted to a double,
% so it can contain values greater than 1.
Ibd=double(Ib);
% STEP 1. Initial labels are assigned
% Variables for labels e and
% for collisions k are initialized
e=2;
k=1;
% Scroll the image from left to right
% and top to bottom
for r=2:m-1
    for c=2:n-1
    % If the neighboring pixels are zero, a label is
assigned
        % and the number of labels is increased.
        if(Ibd(r,c)==1)
            if((Ibd(r,c-1)==0)&&(Ibd(r-1,c)==0))
                Ibd(r,c)=e;
                e=e+1;
            end
    % If one of the neighboring pixels has a tag assigned,
    % this tag is assigned to the current pixel.

if((((Ibd(r,c-1)>1)&&(Ibd(r-1,c)<2))||((Ibd(r,c-
1)<2)&&(Ibd(r-1,c)>1))))
            if(Ibd(r,c-1)>1)
                Ibd(r,c)=Ibd(r,c-1);
            end
        if(Ibd(r-1,c)>1)
                Ibd(r,c)=Ibd(r-1,c);
        end
    end
    end
    % If several of the neighboring pixels have an
assigned label,
        % one of them is assigned to this pixel.
        if((Ibd(r,c-1)>1)&&(Ibd(r-1,c)>1))
            Ibd(r,c)=Ibd(r-1,c);
            % Unused tags are recorded as collision
            if((Ibd(r,c-1))~=(Ibd(r-1,c)))
            ec1(k)=Ibd(r-1,c);
            ec2(k)=Ibd(r,c-1);
```

```
                k=k+1;
              end
          end
        end
     end
end

% STEP 2. Collisions are resolved
for ind=1:k-1
% The smallest label of those participating in the
collision is %detected.
% The group of pixels belonging
% to the smaller label absorb those of the larger label.
    if(ec1(ind)<=ec2(ind))
    for r=1:m
        for c=1:n
            if (Ibd(r,c)==ec2(ind))
                Ibd(r,c)=ec1(ind);
            end
        end
    end
    end
    if(ec1(ind)>ec2(ind))
    for r=1:m
        for c=1:n
            if (Ibd(r,c)==ec1(ind))
                Ibd(r,c)=ec2(ind);
            end
        end
  end
    end
  end
% The unique function returns the values of the array
(Ibd),
% unique, that is, they are not repeated, so they will be
delivered
% only those values that remained when solving the
% collision problem.
w = unique(Ibd);
t=length(w);

% STEP 3. Re-labeling the image
% Pixels with the minimum values are relabeled.
  for r=1:m
        for c=1:n
          for ix=2:t
              if (Ibd(r,c)==w(ix))
                  Ibd(r,c)=ix-1;
```

```
            end
        end
        end
    end
% Prepare data for deployment
E=mat2gray(Ibd);
imshowpair(I,E,'montage');
```

Figure 4.17 shows the labeling of a series of objects contained in a binary image. These results were obtained as a result of the execution of the program in MATLAB shown in 4.3.

4.8 Object Borders in Binary Images

Once the objects have already been labeled in a binary image, the next step could be the extraction of the contour or perimeter of each object. This process would seem to be simple since, at least intuitively, it would imply the registration of the pixels of an object on its border. However, as will be seen in this section, a series of elements are needed for the formulation of this algorithm, whose final objective is to make an organized description of a contour. Determining the contour of binary objects is one of the most frequent tasks in image analysis.

4.8.1 External and Internal Contours

As will be seen in Chapter 10 on morphological operations, it is possible to extract the boundary of binary regions using differences between

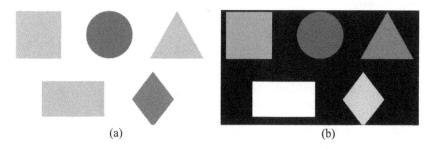

(a)   (b)

FIGURE 4.17
Labeling of objects obtained by the execution of the MATLAB® program 4.3. (a) Original image and (b) labeled image.

morphological operations. However, in this section, the problem is faced from a more advanced perspective since the idea is not only to determine the contour of a binary object but also to order it in a sequence that can be later used to determine different properties. An object can present only an outer contour characterized by pixels that belong to the object, while other elements are in contact with the background of the image. On the other hand, the object can also have different inner contours. These types of artifacts appear due to holes present in the main object as a consequence of a poor segmentation process (see Figure 4.18).

Another extra complication to the contour identification process (see Figure 4.19) occurs when an object becomes thinner to the limit of one pixel and again increases in size. This complication makes it difficult to process the contour since there are pixels that are processed twice in different directions. Therefore, it is not enough to set a starting point from which the contour is identified. It is also necessary to define a direction during the execution.

Next, a combined algorithm will be presented that allows, unlike traditional algorithms, to combine the identification of the contours and the labeling of the objects present in a binary image.

4.8.2 Combination of Contour Identification and Object Labeling

This method integrates the concepts of object labeling and the process of contour identification. The objective is to perform a single execution of both operations. Under this approach, both the outer and inner contours are identified and also labeled. This algorithm does not need any complex data structures for its implementation and is very efficient compared to other similar methods.

The main idea of this algorithm, which is illustrated in Figure 4.20, is simple and considers the following processing steps:

The binary image $I_b(x,y)$, as in the object labeling process, is processed from left to right and from top to bottom. This ensures that all pixels are considered.

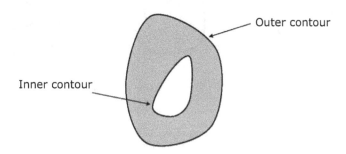

FIGURE 4.18
Binary object with outer and inner contour.

$\mathbf{p}_s$

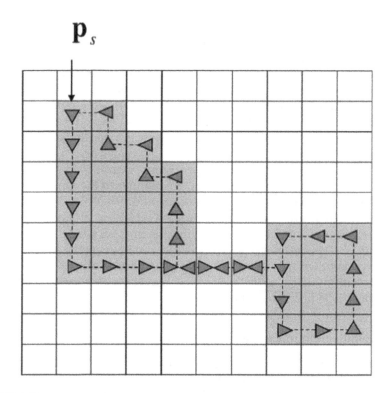

FIGURE 4.19
The trajectory of the contour is represented as an ordered sequence of pixels, considered as a starting point p_s. Pixels can appear on the path more than once.

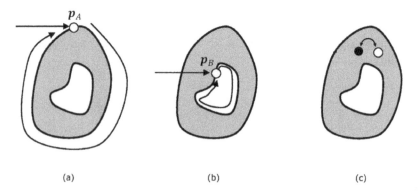

(a)   (b)   (c)

FIGURE 4.20
Combination of contour identification and object labeling. (a) Case when a transition from background to an object occurs, the point is part of the outer boundary; (b) case when the transition from object to background occurs, the pixel is part of the inner boundary; and (c) case of a pixel of the object which is not a contour and assumes the label of its left neighbor.

The following situations may appear in the processing of an image:

Case 1. The transition from the background to a pixel p_A whose value is one and which currently remains unlabeled (Figure 4.20a). When this happens, it means that the p_A pixel is part of the outer contour of the object. Therefore, a new label is assigned to it, and the contour is processed, labeling each of the pixels that belong to it. In addition, all background pixels that are in contact with the object are assigned the value of –1.

Case 2. The transition from a pixel p_B belonging to the object to a background pixel (Figure 4.20b). When this happens, it means that the pixel p_B belongs to an interior contour. Therefore, the contour is processed, labeling the pixels. As in the previous case, the background pixels that are in contact with the object are assigned the value of –1.

Case 3. When a pixel of the object is not part of the contour, in this case, a pixel is labeled with the label value of its left neighbor (Figure 4.20c).

In algorithms 4.2–4.4 the complete process of the algorithm that combines the identification of contours and the labeling process is described. The **LabelOutlineCombination** process goes through the image row by row and calls the **OutlineTrace** function when a pixel belonging to an outer or inner contour is detected. The labeling of a pixel along the contours, as well as the surrounding background pixels, are registered in the structure "Label Map" ME, by calling the **NextNode** function.

ALGORITHM 4.2.   THE ALGORITHM THAT COMBINES THE IDENTIFICATION OF CONTOURS AND LABELING. THE PROCEDURE LABELOUTLINECOMBINATION PRODUCES THE BINARY IMAGE $I_b(x, y)$ A SET OF CONTOURS. WHENEVER A CONTOUR IS LOCATED, THE OUTLINETRACE FUNCTION IS CALLED, WHICH ALLOWS THE CONTOUR TO BE PROCESSED

LabelOutlineCombination $I_b(x, y)$

$I_b(x, y)$, binary image

ME, label map

K, object counter

EA, current label

1:      A set of empty contours $C = \{\ \}$ is created

2:       Create a map of *ME* labels of the same size as $I_b(x,y)$

3:       **for** all pixels (x,y) **do**

4:       $ME(x,y) = 0$

5:       $K = 0$

6:       The image is processed from left to right and from top to bottom.

7:       **for** $y = 1,...,M$ **do**

8:       $EA = 0$

9:              **for** $x = 1,...,N$ **do**

10:                    **if** $(I_b(x,y) = 1)$ **then**

11:                 **if** $(EA \neq 0)$ **then**

12:       $ME(x,y) = EA$

13:       **else**

14:       $EA = ME(x,y)$

15:           **if** $(EA = 0)$ **then**

16:       $K = K + 1$

17:       $EA = K$

18:       $p_s = (x,y)$

19:       $C_{ext} = \text{OutlineTrace}(p_s, 0, EA, I_b(x,y), ME(x,y))$

20:       $C = C \bigcup \{C_{ext}\}$

21:       $ME(x,y) = EA$

22:       **else**

23:           **if** $(L \neq 1)$ **then**

24:       **if** $(ME = 0)$ **then**

25:       $p_s = (x-1,y)$

26: $C_{int} = $ OutlineTrace $(p_s, 0, EA, I_b(x,y), ME(x,y))$

27: $C = C \bigcup \{C_{int}\{\}\}$

28: $L = 0$

Returns (C, ME)

ALGORITHM 4.3. TRACECONTOUR FUNCTION OF THE ALGORITHM. THE FUNCTION PROCESSES THE CONTOUR FROM THE STARTING POINT p_s IN THE DIRECTION $d = 0$ (OUTER CONTOUR) OR $d = 1$ (INNER CONTOUR). IN THIS FUNCTION, THE CONTOUR POINTS ARE REGISTERED

OutlineTrace $p_s, d, L, I_b(x,y), ME(x,y)$

$I_b(x,y)$, binary image

d, search direction

ME, label map

p_s, contour analysis start position

L, outline label

p_T, new contour point

1: An empty contour C is created

2: $(x_T, d) = $ **NextNode** $(p_s, d, I_b(x,y), ME(x,y))$

3: Include p_T to C

4: $p_p = p_s$

5: $p_c = p_T$

6: $p_s = p_T$

7: **while** (**not**($p_s = p_T$)) **do**

8:      $ME(x,y) = L$

9:      $(p_n, d) = \textbf{NextNode}\left(p_c, (d+6)\bmod 8, I_b(x,y), ME(x,y)\right)$

10:      $p_p = p_c$

11:      $p_c = p_n$

12:      temp=$(p_p = p_s \wedge p_c = p_T)$

13:      if (not(temp)) then

14:      Include p_n to C

15:      Returns C

ALGORITHM 4.4. NEXTNODE FUNCTION OF THE ALGORITHM. THE FUNCTION DETERMINES THE NEXT POINT CORRESPONDING TO THE CONTOUR THAT THE OUTLINETRACE FUNCTION PROCESSES DEPENDING ON THE DIRECTION p' IN THE DIRECTION $d = 0$ (EXTERIOR CONTOUR) OR $d = 1$ (INTERIOR CONTOUR)

NextNode $p_c, d, L, I_b(x,y), ME(x,y)$

p_c, original position

d, search direction

$I_b(x,y)$, binary image

ME, label map

$p' = (x', y')$

1:      for $i = 0,...,6$ do

2:      $p' = p_c + \text{DELTA}(d)$

3:      if $I_b(x', y') = 0$ then

4:      $ME(x', y') = -1$

5:     $d = (d+1) \bmod 8$

6:     else

7:         Return (p', d)

8:     Return (p_c, d)

$$DELTA(d) = (\Delta x, \Delta y) \text{ where}$$

d	0	1	2	3	4	5	6	7
Δx	1	1	0	-1	-1	-1	0	1
Δy	0	1	1	1	0	-1	-1	-1

4.8.3 Implementation in MATLAB

This section explains how to implement the program that combines the contour identification and object labeling described in Algorithm 4.1.

First, the algorithm considers, in the processing of the binary image, eliminating the elements outside the image. This makes the processing easier since the outside pixels are not considered neighbors during the execution of the algorithm. Therefore, the processing for an image of dimensions $M \times N$ considers the rows from 2 to $M - 1$ and columns from 2 to $N - 1$.

The algorithm is implemented in Program 4.2. It uses in its operation two functions: OutlineTrace (Program 4.5) and i NextNode (Program 4.6). The **OutlineTrace** function allows you to process the outer and inner contours from a reference point p_s. To do this, the **NextNode** function is called. This function allows you to determine from a point p_s the next point p on the contour trace. If the next point does not exist, which could happen when it is an isolated pixel, the function returns as a response the same p_s point with which the function is called. Therefore, if it is an isolated pixel, the **OutlineTrace** function terminates immediately; if this is not the case, the **NextNode** function is called consecutively as the contour is processed completely.

The **OutlineTrace** function defines the points p_p and p_c on the route, which corresponds to the previous position and the current position, respectively. Therefore, this process ends when $p_c = p_p$, which happens when the procedure has made a complete turnaround in the contour (all elements have been analyzed).

The **NextNode** function determines, from the current point p_c, the next point of the contour. To do this, it will be necessary to specify an initial search direction (d). Starting from this direction, the function performs a search for

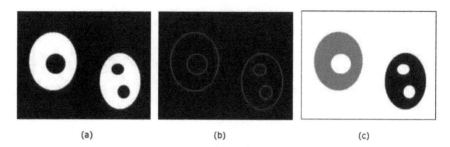

(a)   (b)   (c)

FIGURE 4.21
Results obtained by the algorithm that combines the identification of contours and labeling of objects. (a) Original image, (b) identified contours, and (c) labeled objects.

the next contour pixel in 7 different directions clockwise. These directions are defined in the final part of the table described in Algorithm 4.4. During this process, when it finds a pixel with a value of zero, the label map $ME(x, y)$ assigns the value of –1. With this action, it is avoided going through this pixel again during the search process.

The detected contours are stored in a multidimensional array of the form Co(:,:,NCo), where the first parameters define any size (consistent with the size of the binary image being processed) of the image containing the contour, while NCo indexes the number of contours (Figure 4.21).

PROGRAM 4.4.   IMPLEMENTATION OF THE PROGRAM THAT COMBINES CONTOUR IDENTIFICATION AND OBJECT LABELING IN MATLAB

```
%%%%%%%%%%%%%%%%%%%%%%%%%%%%%%%%%%%%%%%%%%%%%%%%%%%%%%%%%
%Program that implements the combination of the
% Identification of contours and labeling of objects
using
% 8-neighbor neighborhood
%%%%%%%%%%%%%%%%%%%%%%%%%%%%%%%%%%%%%%%%%%%%%%%%%%%%%%%%%

% The binary image is defined as global
% and the label array, such that
% both arrays are accessible and modifiable
% from this program and by functions
% OutlineTrace and NextNode.
global Ib;
global ME;
% Find the size of the binary image
[m n]=size(Ib);
% Consider the matrix of labels with a
% dimension smaller than the original
ME=zeros(m-1,n-1);
```

```
% The contour counter is set to its initial value
cont=1;
% The object counter is set to zero
R=0;
% An image is initialized with zeros that will contain
%the contour objects
C=zeros(m,n);
%The image is processed from left to right and from top
to down

for r=2:m-1
    % The label is initialized to zero
    Lc=0;
    for c=2:n-1
    % If the pixel is one
        if(Ib(r,c)==1)
    % If the label is the same, it is used to label
    % neighboring pixels
            if(Lc~=0)
                ME(r,c)=Lc;
            else
                Lc=ME(r,c);
    % If there is no label, then it is an outer contour
    % so the OutlineTrace function is used
    if(Lc==0)
    % A new object is defined
    R=R+1;
    % The label is reassigned to the object number
    Lc=R;
    % The starting point of the contour is defined
    ps=[r c];
    % call the OutlineTrace function for its processing
    D=OutlineTrace(ps,0,Lc);
    D=im2bw(D);
    % Contours are stored in array Co
    Co(:,:,cont)=D;
    % The final contours are stored in C
    C=D|C;
      cont=cont+1;
      ME(r,c)=Lc;
                    end
                end                 else
                    if(Lc~=0)
        % If label already exists, then it is an inner
contour
        %Then, it is called the function OutlineTrace for
its processing
                if(ME(r,c)==0)
```

```
    % The starting point of the contour is defined
          ps=[r c-1];
    %it is called the function OutlineTrace for its
processing
          D= OutlineTrace(ps,1,Lc);
          D=im2bw(D);
    % Contours are stored in array Co
          Co(:,:,cont)=D;
          C=D|C;
          cont=cont+1;
            end
    % Lc is assigned a non-label definition
                Lc=0;
              end
            end
    end
end

% The label array is reconverted to remove the -1 values
%These values were assigned by the function NextNode.
[m1 n1]=size(ME);
for r=1:m1
    for c=1:n1
        if(ME(r,c)<0)
            ME(r,c)=0;
        end
    end
end
```

PROGRAM 4.5. PROGRAM THAT IMPLEMENTS THE OUTLINETRACE FUNCTION, USED TO PROCESS THE OUTER AND INNER CONTOURS OF OBJECTS CONTAINED IN A BINARY IMAGE. THE FUNCTION IS CALLED BY THE ALGORITHM DESCRIBED IN PROGRAM 4.4

```
%%%%%%%%%%%%%%%%%%%%%%%%%%%%%%%%%%%%%%%%%%%%%%%%%%%%%%%%%%%
% Function used to process and describe the contour
% Either outer or inner of an object. The function
OutlineTrace
%Accessed by program shown in 4.4.
%%%%%%%%%%%%%%%%%%%%%%%%%%%%%%%%%%%%%%%%%%%%%%%%%%%%%%%%%%%

function M= OutlineTrace(ps,d,L)
% The binary image is defined as global
% And the label array, such that
```

```
% Both arrays are accessible and modifiable
% From this program and by functions
% OutlineTrace and NextNode.
global Ib;
global ME;
% Find the size of the binary image
[m1 n1]=size(Ib);
% The matrix M is filled with zeros for storing contours
M=zeros(m1,n1);
% The NextNode function is called,
% Which locates the next pixel in the contour path
[p d]= NextNode(ps,d);
% The point returned by NextNode is put into the matrix M
% Because it is part of the contour
M(p(1),p(2))=1;
% The current point xc and the previous point xp are
defined.
xp=ps;
xc=p;
% If both points are equal, it is an isolated pixel
f=(ps==p);
% The entire contour is traversed until the current point
is equal
% to the previous one, which means that the contour has
been %processed completely.
while(~(f(1)&&f(2)))
    ME(xc(1),xc(2))=L;
    [pn d]= NextNode(xc,mod(d+6,8));
    xp=xc;
    xc=pn;
    f=((xp==ps)&(xc==p));
    if(~(f(1)&&f(2)))
        M(pn(1),pn(2))=1;
    end
end
```

PROGRAM 4.6.   THE PROGRAM THAT IMPLEMENTS THE NEXTNODE FUNCTION USED TO FIND THE NEXT POINT OF THE CONTOUR THAT IS BEING PROCESSED BY THE TRACEOUTLINE FUNCTION

```
%%%%%%%%%%%%%%%%%%%%%%%%%%%%%%%%%%%%%%%%%%%%%%%%%%%%%%%%%%%%
% Function used to find the next contour point
% for an outer or inner object
% The call to the function is made by OutlineTrace %%%%%%
%%%%%%%%%%%%%%%%%%%%%%%%%%%%%%%%%%%%%%%%%%%%%%%%%%%%%
```

```
function [p dir]= NextNode(ps,d1)
% The binary image is defined as global
% And the label array, such that
% Both arrays are accessible and modifiable
% From this program and by functions
% OutlineTrace and NextNode.
global Ib;
global ME;
flag=0;
d=d1;
% The search direction of the following pixel is defined
for j=0:1:6

    if (d==0)
        p(1)=ps(1);
        p(2)=ps(2)+1;
    end
    if (d==1)
        p(1)=ps(1)+1;
        p(2)=ps(2)+1;
    end
    if (d==2)
        p(1)=ps(1)+1;
        p(2)=ps(2);
    end
    if (d==3)
        p(1)=ps(1)+1;
        p(2)=ps(2)-1;
    end
    if (d==4)
        p(1)=ps(1);
        p(2)=ps(2)-1;
    end
    if (d==5)
        p(1)=ps(1)-1;
        p(2)=ps(2)-1;
    end
    if (d==6)
        p(1)=ps(1)-1;
        p(2)=ps(2);
    end
    if (d==7)
        p(1)=ps(1)-1;
        p(2)=ps(2)+1;
    end
    % If the pixel found is part of the background,
```

```
% it is marked with -1 to avoid revisiting it.    if
(Ib(p(1),p(2))==0)
        ME(p(1),p(2))=-1;
        d=mod(d+1,8);
    else
        flag=1;
        break
    end
end
dir=d;
  if (flag==0)
      p(1)=ps(1);
      p(2)=ps(2);
      dir=d1;
  end
```

4.9 Representation of Binary Objects

The most natural way to represent images is by means of a matrix, in which each element of intensity or color corresponds to a position in the matrix. Using this representation, most programming languages can easily and elegantly manipulate images. A possible disadvantage of this representation is that the structure of the image is not considered. That is, it makes no difference whether the image contains a couple of lines or a complex scene, so the amount of memory needed to store it will only depend on its dimensions, not on its content.

Binary objects can be represented as a logical mask, where inside an object will have the value of one and outside the value of zero (Figure 4.22). Because a logical value only needs one bit to be represented, such an array type is called a bitmap.

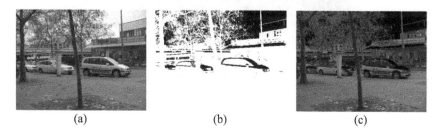

(a)   (b)   (c)

FIGURE 4.22
Use of a binary image as a mask for the specification of regions. (a) Original image, (b) binary mask, and (c) masked image.

4.9.1 Length Encoding

Under this code, pixels are grouped together into blocks and represented by the description of these blocks contained in the image. Therefore, a block is a sequence of pixels whose value is one and that are distributed along either a row or a column. The compact way to represent these blocks is through a vector such that:

$$\text{Block} = \text{row}, \text{column}, \text{length} \qquad (4.11)$$

Figure 4.23 shows an image and its representation under length encoding. This type of representation, as can be seen, is easy and fast to calculate and is even still used as a compression method by the TIFF and GIF formats.

4.9.2 Chain Code

The objects present in an image can be represented not only by describing their area (as was the case for length encoding) but also through their contours. A classic form of this type of representation is the so-called chain encoding or Freeman code. By this method, the contours are represented starting from a reference point p_s as a sequence of numbers that represent

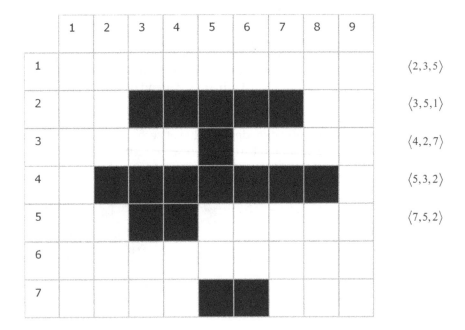

FIGURE 4.23
Length encoding example. This encoding method groups the pixels with a value of one, considering the rows as the grouping direction.

the changes in position through the contour (Figure 4.24). Therefore, for a closed contour defined by the sequence of points $B = (x_1, x_2, ...x_M)$, the corresponding chain code is produced as the sequence $C_C = (c_1, c_2, ..., c_M)$, where:

$$c_i = \text{code}(\Delta x_i, \Delta y_i)$$

$$(\Delta x_i, \Delta y_i) = \begin{cases} (x_{i+1} - x_i, y_{i+1} - y_i) \text{ for } 0 \le i < M \\ (x_1 - x_i, y_1 - y_i) \text{ for } i = M \end{cases} \tag{4.12}$$

and the $\text{code}(\Delta x_i, \Delta y_i)$ is calculated from the data in Table 4.1.

Chain codes are compact in their definition since they specify only the absolute coordinates from a reference point p_s. Furthermore, since the change in position between one point and another is specified by a parameter that has only eight possible values, it is feasible to use only 3 bits to encode each coefficient of the code.

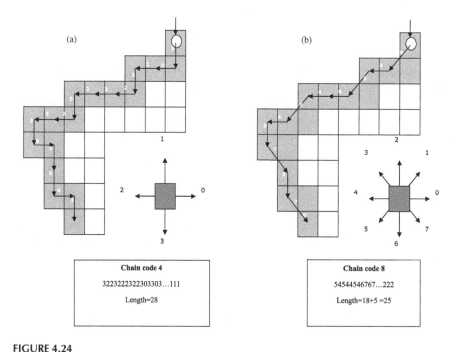

FIGURE 4.24
Chain codes based on the (a) 4-neighbor (a) and 8-neighbor. To calculate the chain codes, it is necessary to process the contour starting from the starting or reference point p_s. The relative position of the neighboring pixels belonging to the contour determines the encoded direction value.

TABLE 4.1

Value Calculation of Code $(\Delta x_i, \Delta y_i)$

Δx_i	1	1	0	−1	−1	−1	0	1
Δy_i	0	1	1	1	0	−1	−1	−1
código $(\Delta x_i, \Delta y_i)$	0	1	2	3	4	5	6	7

4.9.3 Differential Chain Code

Under the representation of chain code, it is not possible to compare two different objects. This is due, first, to the fact that the description is dependent on the starting point p_s. Then, the fact that a 90° rotation produces the description of a totally different contour. One way to solve this issue is through the use of the differential chain code. In this approach, instead of representing the directions of pixels in the contour, the differential chain code registers the changes in direction along the contour. Therefore, for a chain code represented by the sequence $C_C = (c_1, c_2, ..., c_M)$, its differential chain code $C_D = (c'_1, c'_2, ..., c'_M)$ is obtained so that each parameter c_i is calculated as follows:

$$c'_i = \begin{cases} (c_{i+1} - c_i) \bmod 8 \text{ for } 0 \leq i < M \\ (c_1 - c_i) \bmod 8 \text{ for } i = M \end{cases}$$

(4.13)

The determination of each parameter c'_i defined by equation 4.13 considers the 8-neighbor neighborhood criterion. Thus, the element c'_i describes the change of direction between the pixels c_i and c_{i+1} belonging to the contour. Considering this, the representation of the differential chain code of the chain code represented in Figure 4.24(b) is defined as follows:

$$C_C = (5, 4, 5, 4, 4, 5, 4, 6, 7, 6, 7, ..., 2, 2, 2)$$
$$C_D = (7, 1, 7, 0, 1, 7, 2, 1, 7, 1, 1, ..., 0, 0, 3)$$

(4.14)

To reconstruct the contour defined by C_C, it is necessary to know the starting point p_s and its initial direction d, while in the case of C_D, it is not necessary to know anything.

4.9.4 Shape Numbers

The differential chain code can remain invariant to rotations performed on the contours. However, it remains dependent on the starting point from which the code is generated. If we want to compare two different differential codes C_D^1 and C_D^2 of length M, it is necessary to set a common starting point and perform the comparison. A more reliable alternative consists of considering a single value $\text{Val}(C_D)$ calculated from the C_D sequence, where the set of C_D coefficients multiplies a constant parameter B that defines the neighborhood established as a reference. The above could be modeled as follows:

$$\text{Val}(C_D) = c_1 \cdot B^0 + c_2 \cdot B^1 + \ldots + c_M \cdot B^{M-1}$$

$$\text{Val}(C_D) = \sum_{i=1}^{M} c_i \cdot B^{i-1} \tag{4.15}$$

Under such conditions, the C_D sequence can be cyclically shifted until the element k is found at which the value $\text{Val}(C_D)$ produces the maximum. That is:

$$\text{Val}(C_D \to k) = \max \text{ for } 0 \leq k < M \tag{4.16}$$

$C_D \to k$ defines a cyclic displacement of the C_D sequence in k positions to the right. This process is illustrated by the following example:

$$C_D = (1,2,1,3,5,7,\ldots,2,6,5)$$

$$C_D \to 2 = (6,5,1,2,1,3,5,7,\ldots,2) \tag{4.17}$$

These $\text{Val}(C_D \to k) = \max$ values can be considered as normalized sequences and independent from the start or reference point. Therefore, they can be used as a means of comparison between chain sequences. As can be seen in Equation 4.16, the problem is that the calculation of these values results in very large values. Chain comparison cannot be considered a reliable method since the rotations, scaling, or deformations produced in the contours may produce incorrect conclusions.

4.9.5 Fourier Descriptors

An elegant approach to the description of contours is the so-called Fourier descriptors. They consider a set of points that describe the contour of an object $(x_1, x_2, \ldots, x_M)$ where $x_i = (x, y)$ can be described as a sequence of complex numbers $(z_1, z_2, \ldots, z_M)$ where:

$$z_i = x_i + jy \tag{4.18}$$

It is interpreted as a complex number with a real part x and an imaginary part y. From this data sequence, it is possible to construct a one-dimensional periodic function $f(s) \in \mathbb{C}$ that describes the length of a contour. The coefficients of the Fourier transform of the function $f(s)$ allow describing the contour of an object in the frequency domain, where the coefficients corresponding to lower frequencies describe the shape.

4.10 Features of Binary Objects

If you want to describe a binary image to another person, the worst strategy would undoubtedly be to say all the pixels contained in the image and their value, either zero or one. This will only confuse the person. A better way to describe the image would be to use the characteristics of the objects present, such as the number of objects, area, perimeter, etc. Such characteristics can be easily calculated by the computer by manipulating the entire image or a segment of it. In addition, these quantities can be used to discriminate different types of objects, making it possible to use pattern recognition techniques.

4.10.1 Features

A characteristic of a binary object is a certain quantitative measure that can be obtained by direct calculation of its pixels. A simple example of this characteristic is the number of pixels that integrate the object, which can be obtained by simply counting the number of elements that involve the object. To univocally describe an object, several characteristics are normally combined in a vector. This vector represents the signature of the object and can be used for classification purposes. This set of characteristics can be used to discriminate between objects based on the differences that they present in relation to their characteristic vectors. Features, as far as possible, should be robust. This means that they must not be influenced by irrelevant changes, for example, displacement, scaling, and rotation.

4.10.2 Geometric Features

An object O of a binary image can be considered as a distribution of points of value one $x_i = (x, y)$ located on a two-dimensional grid, that is:

$$O = \{x_1, x_2, ..., x_N\} = \{(x_1, y_1), (x_2, y_2), ..., (x_N, y_N)\} \qquad (4.19)$$

For the calculation of most of the geometric characteristics, an object is considered as a set of ones that are grouped under a neighborhood criterion.

4.10.3 Perimeter

The perimeter of an object O is determined by the length of its outer contour. As Figure 4.24 shows, for the calculation of the perimeter, it is necessary to consider the type of neighborhood considered since the distance of the perimeter of a contour under the 4-neighborhood is greater than the 8-neighborhood.

In the case of an 8-neighborhood, a horizontal or vertical movement (see Figure 4.24(b)) has a distance of one, while the diagonal movements have a distance of $\sqrt{2}$. For a contour defined by an 8-neighborhood-based chain code $C_C = (c_1, c_2, ..., c_M)$, the perimeter can be calculated as follows:

$$\text{Perimeter}(O) = \sum_{i=1}^{M} \text{length}(c_i) \tag{4.20}$$

where:

$$\text{length}(c_i) = \begin{cases} 1 & \text{for } c = 0, 2, 4, 6 \\ \sqrt{2} & \text{for } c = 1, 3, 5, 7 \end{cases} \tag{4.21}$$

The perimeter calculated by Equations 4.20 and 4.21 produces a value that overcalculates the true distances. Under such conditions, in practice, this value is normally adjusted. Therefore, the new value of the perimeter defined as $U(O)$ is calculated as follows:

$$U(O) = 0.95 * \text{Perimeter}(O) \tag{4.22}$$

4.10.4 Area

The area of an object O can be calculated simply by summing the pixels that integrate the object. That is:

$$\text{Area}(O) = N = |O| \tag{4.23}$$

When the object whose area needs to be determined is not described by a grouped set of pixels but by the contour that surrounds it, it is possible to approximate the area by the length of its closed exterior contour (only if it does not contain interior contours). Under such conditions, it can be computed as follows:

$$\text{Area}(O) = \frac{1}{2} \cdot \left| \sum_{i=1}^{M} \left(x_i \cdot y_{[(i+1)\bmod M]} - x_{[(i+1)\bmod M]} \cdot y_i \right) \right| \tag{4.24}$$

where x_i and y_i are the coordinates of the points $x_1, ..., x_M$ that are part of the closed contour that involves the object. The contour defined by these points is described by the chain code $C_C = (c_1, c_2, ..., c_M)$. Geometric features such as area and perimeter are robust to displacement and rotation. However, they are highly sensitive to scaling.

4.10.5 Compaction and Roundness

Compaction is defined as the relationship between the area of an object and its perimeter. The perimeter $U(O)$ of an object increases linearly by multiplying by a factor greater than one. On the other hand, the area of an object increases quadratically. Therefore, the compaction $C(O)$ of an object O associates these two terms. It is calculated as follows:

$$C(O) = \frac{\text{Area}(O)}{U^2(O)} \qquad (4.25)$$

This measure is invariant to displacements, rotations, and scaling. The compaction index has a value of $(1/4\pi)$ for a round object of any diameter. Through normalization of the previous factor, the roundness characteristic can be established as:

$$R(O) = 4\pi \frac{\text{Area}(O)}{U^2(O)} \qquad (4.26)$$

$R(O)$ evaluates how an object is similar to a round element. $R(O)$ produces its maximum value (1) when it is a round object, while for other types of objects, the value ranges from 0 to 1. Figure 4.25 shows the roundness values for different types of objects.

4.10.6 Bounding Box

The Bounding Box of an object describes the minimum square that is able to contain it. This rectangle is defined by two points:

$$BB(O) = \left(x_{\min}, x_{\max}, y_{\min}, y_{\max}\right) \qquad (4.27)$$

where $\left(x_{\min}, x_{\max}, y_{\min}, y_{\max}\right)$ represents the maximum and minimum coordinates of each axis that define the rectangle.

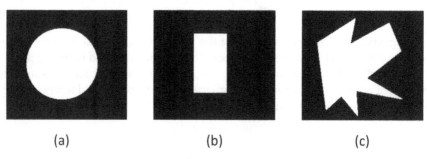

(a)   (b)   (c)

FIGURE 4.25
Roundness value for different objects. (a) 1.00, (b) 0.7415, and (c) 0.4303.

References

[1] L hang, Q., Zhu, X., & Cheng, Y. (2022). An enhanced image segmentation method based on morphological watershed transform. *Journal of Visual Communication and Image Representation*, 97, 104242. doi: https://doi.org/10.1109/ICCIS.2010.69

[2] Jähne, B. (2013). *Digital image processing: Concepts, algorithms, and scientific applications*. Springer.

[3] Burger, W., & Burge, M. J. (2016). *Digital Image Processing*. Springer.

[4] Umbaugh, S. E. (2010). *Digital image processing: Principles and applications*. CRC Press.

[5] Solomon, C., & Breckon, T. (2010). *Fundamentals of digital image processing: A practical approach with examples in MATLAB*. Wiley.

[6] Gose, E., Johnsonbaugh, R., & Jost, S. (2017). *Pattern recognition and image analysis*. CRC Press.

[7] Burger, W., & Burge, M. J. (2010). *Principles of digital image processing: Advanced methods*. Springer.

[8] Jahne, B. (2005). *Digital image processing: Concepts, algorithms, and scientific applicationsss* (4th ed.). Springer.

5

Corner Detection

Corners are defined as prominent points characterized by a high gradient value. However, different from edges, this high gradient value is not only presented in one direction but in distinct orientations [1]. Considering the previous definition, it is possible to visualize the corners as points in the image that belong to different edges at the same time.

The corners can be used in a wide range of applications, such as the tracking of objects in video sequences (tracking), to order the structures of objects in stereoscopic vision, as reference points in the measurement of geometric characteristics of objects, or in the calibration of cameras for vision systems [2]. Some of the advantages of the corners over other characteristics obtained from an image are their robustness to changes in perspective as well as their reliability in their location under different lighting conditions [3].

5.1 Corners in an Image

Considering that corners define a robust and remarkable feature of an image, their localization, as will be seen later, is not easy. An algorithm for corner detection must meet some important aspects, such as:

- Detect "important" corners from "unimportant" ones
- Detect the corners in the presence of noise
- Fast execution to allow its implementation in real-time

As is natural, there are several approaches that are capable of fulfilling these characteristics. Most of these schemes are based on measurements of the gradient at the point that is considered a potential corner. While an edge is defined as a point in the image where the gradient value is especially high but in only one direction, a corner also has high gradient values but in more than one direction simultaneously [4].

The algorithms used for corner detection adopt the criterion of the first or second derivative over the image in the x or y direction as an approximation of the gradient value. A representative algorithm of this class of methods is the Harris Detector. Although there are some other detectors that have

DOI: 10.1201/9781003287414-5

interesting features and properties, the Harris detector is currently the most frequently used method. For this reason, this algorithm is explained in more detail [5].

5.2 The Harris Algorithm

The algorithm developed by Harris and Stephens is based on the idea that a corner is a point in the image where the gradient value shows a high value in several directions simultaneously. This algorithm has the characteristic that it is robust when it classifies between corners and edges. In addition, this detector also presents a high degree of robustness with respect to orientation. Therefore, the corner alignment does not matter [6].

5.2.1 Matrix of Structures

The calculation of the Harris algorithm is based on the expansion of the first partial derivative in a pixel $I(x,y)$ in the horizontal and vertical directions such that:

$$I_x(x,y) = \frac{\partial I(x,y)}{\partial x} \quad y \quad I_y(x,y) = \frac{\partial I(x,y)}{\partial y} \tag{5.1}$$

For each pixel of the image (x,y), three different quantities are calculated that will be called $HE_{11}(x,y)$, $HE_{22}(x,y)$ and $HE_{12}(x,y)$, where:

$$HE_{11}(x,y) = I_x^2(x,y) \tag{5.2}$$

$$HE_{22}(x,y) = I_y^2(x,y) \tag{5.3}$$

$$HE_{12}(x,y) = I_x(x,y) \cdot I_y(x,y) \tag{5.4}$$

These values can be interpreted as approximations of the elements of the matrix of structures defined as HE such that:

$$HE = \begin{bmatrix} HE_{11} & HE_{12} \\ HE_{21} & HE_{22} \end{bmatrix} \tag{5.5}$$

where $HE_{12} = HE_{21}$.

5.2.2 Filtering of the Matrix of Structures

For the location of the corners using the Harris algorithm, it is necessary to smooth the values of each of the elements of the matrix of structures by convolving them through a Gaussian filter H_σ, such that the matrix HE is redefined as the matrix E, such that:

$$E = \begin{bmatrix} HE_{11} * H_\sigma & HE_{12} * H_\sigma \\ HE_{21} * H_\sigma & HE_{22} * H_\sigma \end{bmatrix} = \begin{bmatrix} A & C \\ C & B \end{bmatrix} \tag{5.6}$$

5.2.3 Calculation of Eigenvalues and Eigenvectors

Due to its symmetry, the matrix E can be diagonalized in such a way that:

$$E' = \begin{bmatrix} \lambda_1 & 0 \\ 0 & \lambda_2 \end{bmatrix} \tag{5.7}$$

where λ_1 and λ_2 are the eigenvalues of the matrix E. These values are calculated according to:

$$\lambda_{1,2} = \frac{\text{tr}(E)}{2} \pm \sqrt{\left(\frac{\text{tr}(E)}{2}\right)^2 - \det(E)} \tag{5.8}$$

where $\text{tr}(E)$ implies the trace of the matrix E and $\det(E)$ the determinant of the matrix E. Developing the operations of the trace and determinant of Equation 5.7, we obtain:

$$\lambda_{1,2} = \frac{1}{2}\left(A + B \pm \sqrt{A^2 - 2AB + B^2 + 4C^2}\right) \tag{5.9}$$

Both eigenvalues λ_1 and λ_2 are positive and contain important information about the local structures contained in the image. Within a region of the image whose homogeneous content is a given intensity value, the value of E will be equal to zero ($E = 0$), so the eigenvalues in that region are also $\lambda_1 = \lambda_2 = 0$. However, at an intensity step change with a value of $\lambda_1 > 0$ and $\lambda_2 = 0$, the eigenvalues represent the magnitude of the gradient, while the eigenvectors correspond to the direction. Figure 5.1 shows how the λ_1 and λ_2 values deliver essential information about the structures contained in an image.

A corner point has a high gradient value both in the principal direction, which corresponds to the value of both eigenvalues, and in the direction normal to the principal, which corresponds to the smallest of the eigenvalues. From the above, it can be concluded that for a point to be considered a corner, the eigenvalues λ_1 and λ_2 must have significant values. Since $A, C \geq 0$, it can

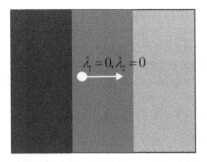 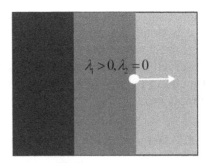

FIGURE 5.1
Relationship of structures in an image and their eigenvalues.

then be seen that $\mathrm{tr}(E) > 0$. With this and observing Equations 5.8 and 5.9, it can be noted that $|\lambda_1| \geq |\lambda_2|$. Considering the above information and the concept that a corner point must have a significant magnitude in both eigenvalues, therefore, for the identification of a corner, only the λ_2 value that is the smallest is considered since if this value is large, then the value of λ_1 will be too.

5.2.4 Corner Value Function (V)

As can be seen from Equations 5.8 and 5.9, the difference between both eigenvalues is established as:

$$\lambda_1 - \lambda_2 = 2 \cdot \sqrt{\left(\frac{\mathrm{tr}(E)}{2}\right)^2 - \det(E)} \tag{5.10}$$

where, in any case, it is true that $(1/4) \cdot \mathrm{tr}(E) > \det(E)$. At a corner point, the difference between the two eigenvalues is small. The Harris algorithm uses this property as significant and implements the function $V(x,y)$ as an index to evaluate the existence of a corner:

$$V(x,y) = \det(E) - \alpha(\mathrm{tr}(E))^2 \tag{5.11}$$

$V(x,y)$ according to Equation 5.6 leads to:

$$V(x,y) = \left(A \cdot B - C^2\right) - \alpha(A + B)^2 \tag{5.12}$$

where the parameter α controls the sensitivity of the algorithm. $V(x,y)$ is defined as the function of the corner value, and the larger its value, the better it characterizes a corner point at (x,y). The value of α is fixed within the interval [0.04, 0.25]. If the value of α is large, it is less sensitive to corner points. For example, if you want to configure the Harris algorithm for higher sensitivity, the value of α should be 0.04. Therefore, it is evident that if α is small, a greater number of corner points will be found in the image. Figure 5.2 shows the value of $V(x,y)$ of an image. From the image, it can be observed how the corner values of the image experience a large value of the function $V(x,y)$, while in the edges and homogeneous regions, the value will simply be almost zero.

5.2.5 Determination of the Corner Points

A pixel (x,y) is considered a potential corner point if the following condition is met:

$$V(x,y) > t_h \tag{5.13}$$

where t_h is the threshold that determines the corner affinity. Its typical value is within the range of 900 to 10,000, depending on the context of the image. Therefore, from the application of Equation 5.13, we will have a binary matrix containing ones (true) where the condition was fulfilled and zeros (false) where it was not valid.

To prevent the location of highly populated regions of corner points, which are calculated due to the high sensitivity of the value α, only those pixels whose value $V(x,y)$ is the largest within a given neighborhood are selected. Figure 5.3 shows an illustration of this process.

FIGURE 5.2
Value of $V(x,y)$ of an image.

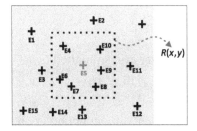

FIGURE 5.3
Process of obtaining the significant corners. For all the corners found by applying the threshold t_h, a defined neighborhood $R(x,y)$ is selected. In this case, the corner value E5 has the maximum value of $V(x,y)$ compared to the other values E4, E6, E7, E8, E9, and E10 that are within the neighborhood region defined by $R(x,y)$. For this reason, E5 is selected as a valid corner.

5.2.6 Algorithm Implementation

Because the Harris algorithm is considered a "complex" process, this section presents a summary of the algorithm and the steps that must be executed to locate the corner points in an image. All the steps are shown in Algorithm 5.1.

ALGORITHM 5.1. HARRIS ALGORITHM FOR CORNER POINT DETECTION

Harris Detector ($I(x,y)$)

1:     Smooth the original image with a prefilter: $I' = I * H_p$

2:     <u>Step 1.</u> Calculate the corner value function $V(x,y)$.

3:     Gradients in the horizontal and vertical directions are calculated.

4:     $I_x = I' * H_x$ and $I_y = I' * H_y$.

5:     The components of the array of structures are computed.

6:     $HE = \begin{bmatrix} HE_{11} & HE_{12} \\ HE_{21} & HE_{22} \end{bmatrix}$

where

7:     $HE_{11}(x,y) = I_x^2(x,y)$

8:     $HE_{22}(x,y) = I_y^2(x,y)$

9:     $HE_{12}(x,y) = I_x(x,y) \cdot I_y(x,y)$

10: where also $HE_{12} = HE_{21}$.

11: Component values are also smoothed by a Gaussian filter.

12: $E = \begin{bmatrix} HE_{11} * H_\sigma & HE_{12} * H_\sigma \\ HE_{21} * H_\sigma & HE_{22} * H_\sigma \end{bmatrix} = \begin{bmatrix} A & C \\ C & B \end{bmatrix}$

13: The value of the corner value function is calculated

14: $V(x,y) = (A \cdot B - C^2) - \alpha(A + B)^2$

15: <u>Step 2.</u> Binarize the value of $V(x,y)$.

16: A binary matrix is obtained by applying the threshold t_h.

17: $U(x,y) = V(x,y) > t_h$

18: Step 3. Significant corner points are located where the binary matrix $S(x,y)$ is constructed, which will contain ones in those pixels that are significant corners and zeros where the corner is not considered as such.

19: A neighborhood region is defined $R(x,y)$.

20: $S(x,y)$ is initialized with all its values zero.

21: **for** all coordinates of the image (x,y) **do**

22: **if** $(U(x,y) == 1)$ **then**

23: **if** $(V(x,y) \geq$ to each of the vectors of $R(x,y))$ **then**

24: $S(x,y) = 1$

25: End **for**

As can be seen from Algorithm 5.1, the original image must be filtered in order to eliminate the possible noise contained in it. In this step, a simple 3×3 low-pass averaging filter can be appropriate. Once the image has been filtered, the gradients of the image are obtained in the horizontal and vertical directions. There are different options that can verify this operation. However, we can use simple filters such as:

$$H_x = \begin{bmatrix} -0.5 & \bar{0} & 0.5 \end{bmatrix} \quad \text{and} \quad H_y = \begin{bmatrix} -0.5 \\ 0 \\ 0.5 \end{bmatrix} \tag{5.14}$$

or Sobel's

$$H_x = \begin{bmatrix} -1 & 0 & 1 \\ -2 & 0 & 2 \\ -1 & 0 & 1 \end{bmatrix} \quad y \quad H_y = \begin{bmatrix} -1 & -2 & -1 \\ 0 & 0 & 0 \\ 1 & 2 & 1 \end{bmatrix} \qquad (5.15)$$

For more details and possibilities of filters to compute the gradient, see Chapter 7. Once we have obtained the values of the gradients, we proceed to calculate the values of the matrix of structures as described in lines 6 to 12 of Algorithm 5.1.

With the calculated values of HE, we proceed to compute E, as illustrated in lines 11 and 12 of Algorithm 5.1, by applying a Gaussian filter. The Gaussian filter, as discussed previously in this book, has a matrix of coefficients as shown in Figure 5.4.

With the value of E, we proceed to obtain the magnitude of the corner value $V(x,y)$ for each pixel according to lines 13 and 14 of the algorithm.

Considering an appropriate value of t_h, the binary matrix $U(x,y)$ is obtained according to lines 16 and 17. At this level of the algorithm, we have in the elements of the matrix $U(x,y)$ the information of those points considered as potential corners since all the elements that are ones will have a value $V(x,y)$ that is greater than the value considered as necessary (t_h). However, due to the sensitivity characteristics of the algorithm (controlled by the parameter α) and the noise contained in the image, there will be several corner points concentrated near a point whose maximum value of $V(x,y)$ will be higher compared to them. To solve this situation, step 3 of the algorithm described in lines 18–25 is implemented. In this part, using the information contained in the matrix $U(x,y)$, the "true corner points" are localized. They are those that experience a maximum value $V(x,y)$ compared to the other corner points

0	1	2	1	0
1	3	5	3	1
2	5	9	5	2
1	3	5	3	1
0	1	2	1	0

FIGURE 5.4
The Gaussian filter for smoothing.

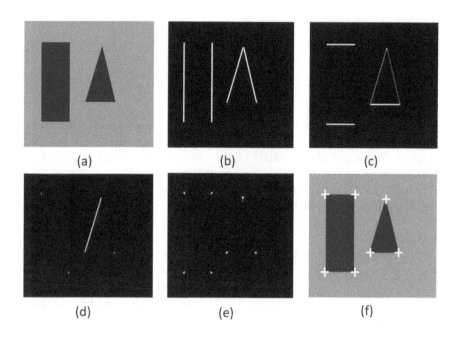

FIGURE 5.5

Application of the Harris algorithm to an artificially generated image with some partial results. (a) Original image, (b) image $I_x^2(x,y)$, (c) image $I_y^2(x,y)$, (d) image $I_x(x,y) \cdot I_y(x,y)$, (e) image of $V(x,y)$, and (f) original image with the location of the "true corner points".

contained in a neighborhood region $R(x,y)$ centered around the test point. Figure 5.5 shows a sequence of images with partial results of the application of Algorithm 5.1 to detect corners on an artificially generated image.

5.3 Determination of Corner Points Using MATLAB

Although MATLAB® offers a function to identify features such as corners, in this section, we will implement the corner detection algorithm directly. The way to program the Harris algorithm will follow the steps indicated in Algorithm 5.1. Program 5.1 shows the MATLAB code that fully implements the Harris operator.

Next, some important aspects that must be considered in the programming of the Harris algorithm will be discussed. The first interesting aspect occurs when the arrays $U(x,y)$ as well as $S(x,y)$ are initialized with zeros. This action is a standard situation in those applications where pixels with some special characteristics are located, which in quantity will obviously be much less compared to the size of the image.

PROGRAM 5.1. MATLAB IMPLEMENTATION
OF THE HARRIS ALGORITHM

```
%%%%%%%%%%%%%%%%%%%%%%%%%%%%%%%%%%%%%%%%%%%%%%%%%%%%%%%%%
% Implementation of the Harris algorithm
% for corner detection in an image
%%%%%%%%%%%%%%%%%%%%%%%%%%%%%%%%%%%%%%%%%%%%%%%%%%%%%%%%%
I=imread('fig.jpg');
Ir=rgb2gray(I);
%The size of the image Ir is obtained to which
%the corners will be extracted (STEP 1).
[m,n]=size(Ir);
%Arrays U and S are initialized with zeros
U=zeros(size(Ir));
S=zeros(size(Ir));
% Prefilter coefficient matrix is created %smoothing
h=ones(3,3)/9;
%The original image's datatype is changed to double
Id=double(Ir);
%The image is filtered with the average h filter.
If=imfilter(Id,h);
%The coefficient matrices are generated to
%calculate the horizontal gradient Hx and vertical
gradient Hy
Hx=[-0.5 0 0.5];
Hy=[-0.5;0;0.5];
%Horizontal and vertical gradients are calculated
Ix=imfilter(If,Hx);
Iy=imfilter(If,Hy);
%The coefficients of the matrix of structures are
obtained
HE11=Ix.*Ix;
HE22=Iy.*Iy;
HE12=Ix.*Iy; %y HE21
%The Gaussian filter matrix is created
Hg=[0 1 2 1 0; 1 3 5 3 1;2 5 9 5 2;1 3 5 3 1;0 1 2 1 0];
Hg=Hg*(1/57);
%Structure matrix coefficients are filtered
%with the Gaussian filter
A=imfilter(HE11,Hg);
B=imfilter(HE22,Hg);
C=imfilter(HE12,Hg);
%Set alpha value to 0.1 (Medium Sensitivity)
alpha=0.1;
%Get the magnitude of the corner value
Rp=A+B;  %Partial result
Rp1=Rp.*Rp;   %Partial result
%Corner value (Q matrix)
```

```
Q=((A.*B)-(C.*C))-(alpha*Rp1);
%Threshold value is set
th=1000;
%The matrix U is obtained (STEP 2).
U=Q>th;
%Set the value of the neighborhood
pixel=10;
%The largest value of Q is obtained,
%of a neighborhood defined by the pixel variable (STEP 3)
for r=1:m
for c=1:n
        if(U(r,c))
            %The left boundary of the neighborhood is
defined
            I1=[r-pixel 1];
            %The right boundary of the neighborhood is
defined
            I2=[r+pixel m];
            %The upper limit of the neighborhood is
defined
            I3=[c-pixel 1];
            %The lower limit of the neighborhood is
defined
            I4=[c+pixel n];
            %The positions are defined considering that
their values are relative to r and c.
            datxi=max(I1);
            datxs=min(I2);
            datyi=max(I3);
            datys=min(I4);
            matrix Q is extracted
            Bloc=Q(datxi:1:datxs,datyi:1:datys);
            %The maximum value of the neighborhood is
obtained
            MaxB=max(max(Bloc));
            %If the current value of the pixel is the
maximum
            %then a 1 is placed in that position in the S
matrix.
            If(Q(r,c)==MaxB)
                S(r,c)=1;
            end
        end
    end
end
%The original image is displayed I
figure
imshow(I);
```

```
%The graphic object is maintained
%so that the other graphic commands have an effect on the
displayed image.
Hold on
%The calculated corners with the Harris algorithm are
drawn over the image
%Ir in the positions where 1s exist within matrix S
for r=1:m
    for c=1:n
        if(S(r,c))
        %Where there's a 1, a + symbol is added to de Ir
image.
        Plot(c,r,'+','MarkerSize',8);
        end
    end
end
```

Considering the above, it is much more practical and faster to initialize the arrays with zeros and place elements inside that meet a certain property. The implemented smoothing prefilter is a "Box" type filter, with a mask of 3×3, while the filters used to calculate the gradients are those defined in Equation 5.14. All operations performed between images and filters in Program 5.1 are performed by the MATLAB imfilter function discussed in detail in previous sections of this book.

The operations executed for the calculation of the elements of the matrix of structures, as they are element-by-element processes, are carried out by applying the MATLAB dot operator, that is, considering the expressions

$$A * B \tag{5.16}$$

$$A. * B \tag{5.17}$$

The first (5.16) implies matrix multiplication between the images A and B, while the second (5.17) defines point-to-point multiplication between all the elements of the matrices A and B.

Another important part of Program 5.1 is represented by step 3. It integrates the necessary instructions for selecting the pixels whose $V(x,y)$ value is maximum within a region. To program this procedure, the image is sequentially processed pixel by pixel, finding the maximum value of a neighborhood block or region established around the point in question. To do this, the limits of the block are set relative to the pixel position in question. In the case of Program 5.1, the interval is set equal to 10. Therefore, considering both directions, the total size is 20. Once the limits are established, the block is extracted, and the maximum value is found. If the maximal value of the block corresponds to the central pixel of the block, then a one is set in position $S(x,y)$. Therefore, the ones in $S(x,y)$ represent the corner points found in the image. Figure 5.3 shows the process of finding the maximum value within the considered neighborhood around the point in question.

Once the points are stored in $S(x,y)$, they are plotted. To carry out this process, the image is first displayed using the well-known display function used by MATLAB: imshow. Then, using the hold on command, the image is maintained, and the points are drawn on it one by one using the plot command, placing a plus sign + at each point. Figure 5.6 shows the location of the corner points detected once Program 5.1 has been executed on an example image.

(a)

(b)

FIGURE 5.6
Location of the corner points according to the Harris algorithm. (a) Original image, (b) Image with corner points located for a value of $\alpha = 0.1$

5.4 Other Corner Detectors

In this section, some other existing detectors that allow finding corners of an image will be analyzed. Among the approaches analyzed are the Beaudet operator, Kitchen & Rosenfeld, and Wang & Brady [7]. All the operators considered here are based on the computation of the Hessian matrix or the Hessian. For this reason, it is necessary to analyze certain details about this matrix.

The Hessian matrix of a function f of n variables is a $n \times n$ square matrix that integrates the second partial derivatives of f. So given a real function f of two real variables:

$$f = (x, y) \tag{5.18}$$

If all second partial derivatives of f exist, the Hessian matrix of f is defined as:

$$H_f(x, y) \tag{5.19}$$

where

$$H_f(x, y) = \begin{bmatrix} \dfrac{\partial^2 f(x,y)}{\partial x^2} & \dfrac{\partial^2 f(x,y)}{\partial x \partial y} \\ \dfrac{\partial^2 f(x,y)}{\partial x \partial y} & \dfrac{\partial^2 f(x,y)}{\partial y^2} \end{bmatrix} \tag{5.20}$$

The components of the Hessian are defined as:

$$I_{xx} = \frac{\partial^2 f(x,y)}{\partial x^2} \tag{5.21}$$

$$I_{yy} = \frac{\partial^2 f(x,y)}{\partial y^2} \tag{5.22}$$

$$I_{xy} = \frac{\partial^2 f(x,y)}{\partial x \partial y} \tag{5.23}$$

5.4.1 Beaudet Detector

The Beaudet detector is an isotropic operator based on the calculation of the determinant of the Hessian. Therefore, if the Hessian is defined by Equation 5.20, its determinant is computed as follows:

$$\det\left(H_f\left(x,y\right)\right) = I_{xx}I_{yy} - I_{xy}^2 \tag{5.24}$$

Based on the calculation of the determinant, the Beaudet detector is defined as:

$$B(x,y) = \frac{\det(H_f\left(x,y\right))}{\left(1 + I_x^2 + I_y^2\right)^2} \tag{5.25}$$

where I_x and I_y are defined as follows:

$$I_x = \frac{\partial f\left(x,y\right)}{\partial x} \quad y \quad I_y = \frac{\partial f\left(x,y\right)}{\partial y} \tag{5.26}$$

Similar to the gradients, under this operator, the points from $B(x,y)$ that exceed a certain predetermined threshold will be considered corners. Program 5.2 shows the MATLAB program that fully implements the Beaudet detector.

PROGRAM 5.2. IMPLEMENTATION IN MATLAB OF THE BEAUDET ALGORITHM

```
%%%%%%%%%%%%%%%%%%%%%%%%%%%%%%%%%%%%%%%%%%%%%%%%%%%%%%%%%%%%%%
% Implementation of the Beaudet algorithm
% for corner detection in an image
%%%%%%%%%%%%%%%%%%%%%%%%%%%%%%%%%%%%%%%%%%%%%%%%%%%%%%%%%%%%%%
%The image is loaded to detect the corners.
Iorig = imread('fig8-6.jpg');
%It is then converted to datatype double
%to prevent calculation issues
Im = double(rgb2gray(Iorig));
%The prefilter matrix is defined
h=ones(3)/9;
%The image is filterd
Im = imfilter(Im,h);
%The Sobel filters are defined
sx=[-1,0,1;-2,0,2;-1,0,1];
sy=[-1,-2,-1;0,0,0;1,2,1];
%The first partial derivative is obtained
Ix = imfilter(Im,sx);
Iy = imfilter(Im,sy);

%The second partial derivative is obtained
Ixx = imfilter(Ix,sx);
Iyy = imfilter(Iy,sy);
Ixy = imfilter(Ix,sy);
```

```
%The denominator of 8.25 is calculated
B = (1 +Ix.* Ix + Iy.* Iy) .^2;
%We obtain the determinant defined in 8.24
A = Ixx.*Iyy - (Ixy).^2;
%Calculate the value of B(x,y) of 8.25
B = (A./B);
%The image is scaled
B=( 1000/max(max(B)))*B;
%The image is binarized
V1= (B)>80;
%The search neighborhood is defined
pixel = 80;
%The largest value of B is obtained from a
%neighborhood defined by the pixel variable
[n,m] = size(V1);
res = zeros(n,m);
for r=1:n
    for c=1:m
        if (V1(r,c))
            I1=[r-pixel,1];
            I1 =max(I1);
            I2=[r+pixel,n];
            I2=min(I2);
            I3=[c-pixel,1];
            I3 =max(I3);
            I4=[c+pixel,m];
            I4=min(I4);

            tmp = B(I1:I2,I3:I4);
            maxim = max(max(tmp));
            if(maxim == B(r,c))
                res(r,c) = 1;
            end
        end
    end
end
%The calculated corners are drawn over the
%Iorig image in the positions where 1s
%are present within the res matrix
imshow(uint8(Iorig));
hold on
[re,co] = find(res');
plot(re,co,'+');
```

Figure 5.7 shows the corners detected in an example image using the Beaudet algorithm. For didactical reasons, in the following examples, the same image will be used for analysis and comparison purposes.

FIGURE 5.7
Location of corner points according to Beaudet's algorithm.

5.4.2 Kitchen & Rosenfield Detector

Kitchen & Rosenfeld proposed a corner detector based on the change of gradient. Under such conditions, the Kitchen and Rosenfeld detector can be computed using the following model:

$$KR(x,y) = \frac{I_{xx} \cdot I_y^2 + I_{yy} \cdot I_x^2 - 2 \cdot I_{xy} \cdot I_y}{I_x^2 + I_y^2} \tag{5.27}$$

In this approach, the corners are considered as those values that exceed a predetermined value considered as a threshold. Program 5.3 shows the MATLAB program that fully implements the Kitchen & Rosenfeld operator.

**PROGRAM 5.3.   IMPLEMENTATION IN MATLAB
OF THE KITCHEN & ROSENFELD ALGORITHM**

```
%%%%%%%%%%%%%%%%%%%%%%%%%%%%%%%%%%%%%%%%%%%%%%%%%%%%%%%%%%%%
% Implementation of the Kitchen and Rosenfeld algorithm
% for corner detection in an image.
%%%%%%%%%%%%%%%%%%%%%%%%%%%%%%%%%%%%%%%%%%%%%%%%%%%%%%%%%%%%
%The image is loaded to detect the corners.
Iorig = imread('fig8-6.jpg');
%It is then converted to datatype double
%to prevent calculation issues
Im = double(rgb2gray(Iorig));
%The prefilter matrix is defined
h=ones(3)/9;
```

```
%The image is filterd
Im = imfilter(Im,h);
%The Sobel filters are defined
sx=[-1,0,1;-2,0,2;-1,0,1];
sy=[-1,-2,-1;0,0,0;1,2,1];
%The first partial derivative is obtained
Ix = imfilter(Im,sx);
Iy = imfilter(Im,sy);
%The second partial derivative is obtained
Ixx = imfilter(Ix,sx);
Iyy = imfilter(Iy,sy);
Ixy = imfilter(Ix,sy);
%The numerator of equation 7.27 is calculated
A = (Ixx.*(Iy.^2)) + (Iyy.*(Ix.^2))- (2*Ixy.*Iy);
%The denominator of equation 7.27 is calculated
B = (Ix.^2) + (Iy.^2);
%Equation 7.27 is calculated
V = (A./B);
%The image is scaled
V=( 1000/max(max(V)))*V;
%The image is binarized
V1= (V)>40;
%The search neighborhood is defined
pixel = 10;
%The maximum value of V is obtained
%from a neighborhood defined by the pixel variable
[n,m] = size(V1);
res = zeros(n,m);
for r=1:n     %rows
    for c=1:m %cols
        if (V1(r,c))
            I1=[r-pixel,1];
            I1 =max(I1);
            I2=[r+pixel,n];
            I2=min(I2);
            I3=[c-pixel,1];
            I3 =max(I3);
            I4=[c+pixel,m];
            I4=min(I4);

            tmp = V(I1:I2,I3:I4);
            maxim = max(max(tmp));
            if(maxim == V(r,c))
               res(r,c) = 1;
            end
        end
    end
end
```

```
%The calculated corners are drawn over the Iorig image
%in the positions where there are 1s in the res matrix
imshow(uint8(Iorig));
hold on
[re,co] = find(res');
plot(re,co,'+');
```

Figure 5.8 shows the corners detected in an example image using the Kitchen & Rosenfeld algorithm.

5.4.3 Wang & Brady Detector

The Wang & Brady operator for corner detection considers an image as a surface. Under such conditions, the algorithm searches for places in the image where the direction of an edge changes abruptly. To do this, a coefficient $C(x,y)$ is defined where the change of direction is evaluated under the following expression:

$$C(x,y) = \nabla^2 I(x,y) + c\left|\nabla I(x,y)\right| \tag{5.28}$$

where c represents a parameter that calibrates the sensitivity of the algorithm. While $\nabla^2 I(x,y)$ and $\nabla I(x,y)$ are defined as:

FIGURE 5.8
Location of the corner points according to the Kitchen & Rosenfeld algorithm.

$$\nabla^2 I(x,y) = \frac{\partial^2 I(x,y)}{\partial x^2} + \frac{\partial^2 I(x,y)}{\partial y^2}$$

(5.29)

$$\nabla I(x,y) = \frac{\partial I(x,y)}{\partial x} + \frac{\partial I(x,y)}{\partial y}$$

Therefore, to detect whether a pixel is a corner or not, it is considered a threshold. Under such circumstances, if a pixel fulfills the conditions imposed by the threshold, it is considered as a corner. Otherwise, it is not a corner. Using the derivative approximation defined in Equation 7.2 (mentioned in Chapter 7), it can be established that:

$$\frac{\partial I(x,y)}{\partial x} = -0.5I(x-1,y) + 0.5(x+1,y)$$

$$\frac{\partial I(x,y)}{\partial y} = -0.5I(x,y-1) + 0.5(x,y+1)$$

(5.30)

Therefore, the operator $\nabla I(x,y)$ is redefined, such that:

$$\nabla I(x,y) = -0.5I(x-1,y) + 0.5I(x+1,y) - 0.5I(x,y-1) + 0.5I(x,y+1)$$

$$\nabla I(x,y) = \begin{bmatrix} 0 & -0.5 & 0 \\ -0.5 & 0 & 0.5 \\ 0 & 0.5 & 0 \end{bmatrix}$$

(5.31)

Similarly, it is established in Equations 7.29 and 7.30 of Chapter 7 that:

$$\frac{\partial^2 I(x,y)}{\partial x^2} = I(x+1,y) - 2I(x,y) + I(x-1,y)$$

$$\frac{\partial^2 I(x,y)}{\partial y^2} = I(x,y+1) - 2I(x,y) + I(x,y-1)$$

(5.32)

So that:

$$\nabla^2 I(x,y) = I(x+1,y) + I(x-1,y) + I(x,y+1) + I(x,y-1) - 4I(x,y)$$

$$\nabla^2 I(x,y) = \begin{bmatrix} 0 & 1 & 0 \\ 1 & -4 & 1 \\ 0 & 1 & 0 \end{bmatrix}$$

(5.33)

Program 5.4 shows the MATLAB program that fully implements the Wang & Brady operator.

PROGRAM 5.4. IMPLEMENTATION IN MATLAB OF THE WANG & BRADY ALGORITHM

```
%%%%%%%%%%%%%%%%%%%%%%%%%%%%%%%%%%%%%%%%%%%%%%%%%%%%%%%%%%%
% Implementation of the Wang and Brady algorithm
% for corner detection in an image
%%%%%%%%%%%%%%%%%%%%%%%%%%%%%%%%%%%%%%%%%%%%%%%%%%%%%%%%%%%
%The image is loaded to detect the corners.
Iorig = imread('fig8-6.jpg');
%It is then converted to datatype double
%to prevent calculation issues
Im = double(rgb2gray(Iorig));
%The prefilter matrix is defined
h=ones(3)/9;
%The image is filtered
Im = imfilter(Im,h);
%The filter described in equation 8.31 is defined
d1=[0,-0.5,0;-0.5,0,0.5;0,0.5,0];
%The filter described in equation 8.33 is defined
d2=[0,1,0;1,-4,1;0,1,0];
%Expressions 8.31 and 8.33 are calculated
I1 = imfilter(Im,d1);
I2 = imfilter(Im,d2);
%Sensitivity parameter is defined
c= 4;
%The Wang and Brady operator Eq. 8.28 is calculated
V = (I2 - c*abs(I1));
%The image is scaled
V=( 1000/max(max(V)))*V;
%The image is binarized
V1= (V)>250;
%The search neighborhood is defined
pixel = 40;
%The maximum value of V is obtained
%from a neighborhood defined by the pixel variable
[n,m] = size(V1);
res = zeros(n,m);
for r=1:n
    for c=1:m
        if (V1(r,c))
            I1=[r-pixel,1];
            I1 =max(I1);
            I2=[r+pixel,n];
            I2=min(I2);
            I3=[c-pixel,1];
```

```
            I3 =max(I3);
            I4=[c+pixel,m];
            I4=min(I4);

            tmp = V(I1:I2,I3:I4);
            maxim = max(max(tmp));
            if(maxim == V(r,c))
               res(r,c) = 1;
            end
         end
      end
end
%The calculated corners are drawn over the Iorig image
%in the positions where there are 1s in the res matrix
imshow(uint8(Iorig));
hold on
[re,co] = find(res');
plot(re,co,'+');
```

Figure 5.9 shows the corners detected in an example image using the Wang & Brady algorithm.

In order to show a comparative vision of the operators considered in this section, Figure 5.10 shows the application of the different algorithms: Harris, Beaudet, Kitchen & Rosenfeld, and Wang & Brady.

FIGURE 5.9
Location of the corner points according to the Wang & Brady algorithm.

FIGURE 5.10
Comparison of algorithms for corner detection: +Harris, o Beaudet, x Kitchen & Rosenfeld, and □ Wang & Brady.

References

[1] Acharya, T., & Ray, A. K. (2017). *Image processing: Principles and applications*. CRC Press.

[2] Umbaugh, S. E. (2017). *Digital image processing and analysis: Human and computer vision applications with CVIPtools* (2nd ed.). CRC Press.

[3] Russ, J. C. (2011). *The image processing handbook* (6th ed.). CRC Press.

[4] McAndrew, A. (2017). *Introduction to digital image processing with MATLAB*. CRC Press.

[5] Chen, J., Zou, L. H., Zhang, J., & Dou, L. H. (2009). The comparison and application of corner detection algorithms. *Journal of Multimedia*, 4(6), 435–441.

[6] Ye, Z., Pei, Y., & Shi, J. (2009). An improved algorithm for Harris corner detection. In *2009 2nd International Congress on Image and Signal Processing* (pp. 1–4). IEEE.

[7] Mehrotra, R., Nichani, S., & Ranganathan, N. (1990). Corner detection. *Pattern Recognition*, 23(11), 1223–1233.

6

Line Detection

6.1 Structures in an Image

An intuitive approach to finding structures in an image could consist of starting from a certain point belonging to an edge, step by step adding the pixels belonging to the entire edge, and with them determining the structure. The previous approximation can be tried both on images from gradient thresholding as well as images from segmentation. This approximation, however, will fail as it does not consider the fractures and ramifications in the edges due to the noise and the uncertainty inherent to the algorithms for calculating the gradient or the segmentation that do not incorporate any kind of criteria on the shapes that are sought in the image [1].

A totally different approach is the global search for structures present in the image that somehow approximate or relate to a previously specified type of form. As can be seen in Figure 6.1, to the eyes of a human, the types of structures present in the images are clearly distinguishable, despite the large number of added points. Until now, the responsible biological mechanism that allows relating and recognizing structures in the images perceived by humans or animals has been unknown. A technique that allows, at least

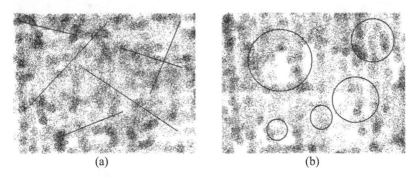

(a)　　　　　　　　　　　　(b)

FIGURE 6.1
Existing biological mechanisms in humans allow geometric parametric structures to be clearly identified without uncertainty, despite the set of points added as noise to the images (a) and (b).

DOI: 10.1201/9781003287414-6

from the computational point of view, to solve this problem is the so-called Hough transform [2], which will be treated in detail in this chapter.

6.2 Hough Transform

The Hough Transform method, devised by Paul Hough and patented in the United States of America, is commonly known in the vision community as the Hough Transform [3]. This transform allows locating parametric shapes from a distribution of points present in an image [4]. Parametric shapes are lines, circles, or ellipses, which can be described by using a few parameters. Because these types of objects (lines, circles, and ellipses), as shown in Figure 6.2, are frequently presented in images, it is especially important to find them automatically.

In this chapter, the use of the Hough Transform will be analyzed for the detection of lines on binary images produced by gradient thresholding because this is a frequent application in many vision or image processing systems [5], and it is also the case introduction that allows to analyze the capacities of this transform. A line in a two-dimensional space is described by using two real parameters expressed in Equation 6.1,

FIGURE 6.2
Parametric figures such as lines, circles, or ellipses are frequently present in images.

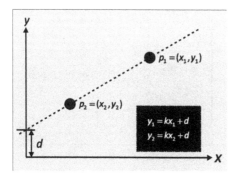

FIGURE 6.3
Two points p_1 and p_2 that belong to the same line, to determine the equation of the line, it will be necessary to estimate the values k and d.

$$y = kx + d \qquad (6.1)$$

where k represents the slope and the point of the axis where the line intercepts it (see Figure 6.3). A line that passes through two different points $p_1 = (x_1, y_1)$ and $p_2 = (x_2, y_2)$ must satisfy the following conditions:

$$y_1 = kx_1 + d \quad y \quad y_2 = kx_2 + d \qquad (6.2)$$

where $k, d \in \Re$. The objective, therefore, is to estimate the parameters k and d of a line that passes through different points belonging to the edges of an object. Faced with this situation, the question arises: How can it be determined what possible points a line encompasses? A possible approach would be to draw all the possible lines in an image and count exactly the points that pass over each one of them, and then delete all those lines that do not contain more than a certain number of points. The above is possible, however, because the number of possible lines that would be drawn on the image is very large, which would make it especially inefficient.

6.2.1 Parameter Space

The Hough Transform solves the line detection problem in a slightly different way: by producing all possible lines that pass through a pixel that corresponds to an edge of the image [6]. Each line L_p that passes through a point $p_0 = (x_0, y_0)$ has the following equation:

$$L_p : y_0 = kx_0 + d \qquad (6.3)$$

where the values of k and d are varied to draw all the possible lines that have x_0 and y_0 in common. The set of solutions for k and d of Equation 6.3 corresponds to an infinite number of lines that pass through the points x_0 and y_0

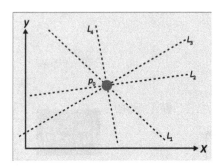

FIGURE 6.4
Set of lines that pass through a common point p_0. All possible lines L_p passing through p_0 have the expression $y_0 = kx_0 + d$ where the values k and d are variables and determine the difference between each of the defined lines.

(see Figure 6.4). For a given value of k, the corresponding solution of 6.3 is produced as a function of d, which would imply:

$$d = y_0 - kx_0 \qquad (6.4)$$

This represents a linear function, where k and d are the variables and x_0 and y_0 are the constants of the parameters considered in the function. The solution set $\{(k,d)\}$ of Equation 6.4 describes the parameters of all possible lines that pass through the point $p_0 = (x_0, y_0)$.

For a given pixel of the image $p_i = (x_i, y_i)$, according to Equation 8.4, there is a set of straight lines defined by:

$$R_i : d = y_i - kx_i \qquad (6.5)$$

Having as variable parameters k and d which define the parameter space also called the Hough space, while x_i and y_i are the fixed parameters also called the image parameter space. The way in which both spaces are related is summarized in Table 6.1.

Each point p_i in the image parameter space corresponds to a line in the Hough parameter space. Considering the above, we are interested in those

TABLE 6.1

Fields of the Structure Returned by the houghlines Function

Field	Description
point1	It is a 2-element vector (x,y) that specifies the start of the segment.
point2	It is a 2-element vector (x,y) that specifies the end of the segment.
Theta	Vector containing information on how linearly the parameter θ was divided.
rho	Vector containing information on how linearly the parameter r was divided.

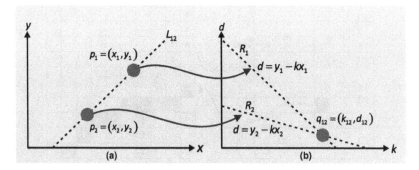

FIGURE 6.5
Relationship between the image parameter space and the Hough parameter space. (a) Image parameter space and (b) Hough parameter space. Points in the parameter space correspond to lines in the Hough parameter space, while the reverse is also true, a point in the Hough parameter space corresponds to a line in the image parameter space. In the image, the points p_1 and p_2 of the image parameter space correspond to the lines R_1 and R_2 in the Hough parameter space; likewise, the point $q_{12}=(k_{12}, d_{12})$ the Hough parameter space corresponds to the line L_{12} of the image parameter space.

points where the lines established in the Hough parameter space intersect, which will correspond to the values of k and d that represent the line of the image space that passes through the points that formulated the lines in the Hough parameter space. As shown in Figure 6.5, the lines R_1 and R_2 intersect at the point $q = (k_{12}, d_{12})$ in the Hough parameter space, which represent the points p_1 and p_2 in the parameter space of the image. So, the line in the image space will have a slope of k_{12} and an intercept point on the y-axis of d_{12}. The more lines in the Hough parameter space that intersect mean that the line in the image space will be made up of that number of points. So, it could be established that:

If NR is the number of lines that intersect in $\left(\bar{k},\bar{d}\right)$ of the Hough parameter space, then there will be NR points that lie on the line defined by $y = \bar{k}x + \bar{d}$ in the image space.

6.2.2 Accumulation Records Matrix

The method for locating lines in an image is based on finding the coordinates in the Hough parameter space where several lines are cut. To calculate the Hough transform, it is first necessary to discretize in a stepped manner the range of values corresponding to k and d. When counting cuts produced by the intersection of several lines in the Hough parameter space, an accumulation records matrix is used, where each cell is increased based on the number of lines that pass through that cell. In such a way that the final number N_p stored in the register would mean that this specific line is made up of N_p pixels of the image parameter space. Figure 6.6 illustrates this process considering the one taken in Figure 6.5 as an example.

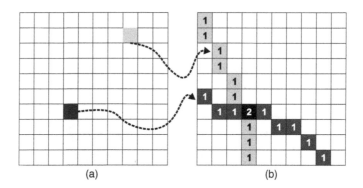

(a)   (b)

FIGURE 6.6

Fundamental idea of the Hough transform. (a) Image parameter space and (b) accumulator in Hough parameter space. As can be seen, the accumulation register matrix is the discretized version of the Hough parameter space. For each point in the parameter space of image (a), there is a line in the Hough parameter space. The operation that is carried out is additive, which means that each cell of the matrix is increased by a value of one as a line passes through it. In this way, the points that maintain a local maximum in the Hough parameter space represent the k and d values that represent the lines in the image parameter space.

6.2.3 Parametric Model Change

So far, the basic idea of the Hough transform has been shown. However, the representation of the straight line defined in Equation 6.1 cannot be used due to the computational error caused in the vertical lines where $k = \infty$. A better option represents the use of the equation:

$$x \cdot \cos(\theta) + y \cdot \sin(\theta) = r \tag{6.6}$$

which does not present any singularity and also allows a linear quantification of its parameters r and θ. Figure 6.7 illustrates the singularity problem in Equation 6.1 and shows how to relate Equation 6.6 to the line problem. With the use of Equation 6.6 for the description of lines, the Hough parameter space varies. So, the parameter space of the coordinates r and θ and the point $p_i = (x_i, y_i)$ of the image parameter space are related according to the equation:

$$r_{x_i, y_i} = x_i \cdot \cos(\theta) + y_i \cdot \sin(\theta) \tag{6.7}$$

where the range of values for θ is $0 \leq \theta < \pi$ (see Figure 6.8). If the center of the image (x_c, y_c) is used as a reference point to define image pixel coordinates (so that these could be positive and negative indices for both x and y), then the range of values of r is restricted to half being defined by:

$$-rx, y_{\max\max} \tag{6.8}$$

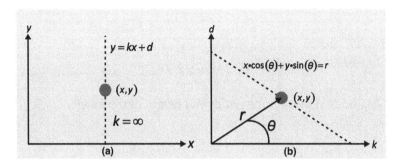

FIGURE 6.7
Different types of parameters that can be used to characterize lines. Option (a) shows the singularity for when trying to characterize a vertical line; in that case $k = \infty$, when choosing the characterization of lines by this type of parameter, any type of line could be represented except those close to the vertical position. A better approach would be the use of Equation 6.6, which, in addition to not showing the singularity, allows a linear quantification of its parameters, where the relationship between the line and the parameters is characterized in (b), with the referred line being the normal to the vector defined by r and θ.

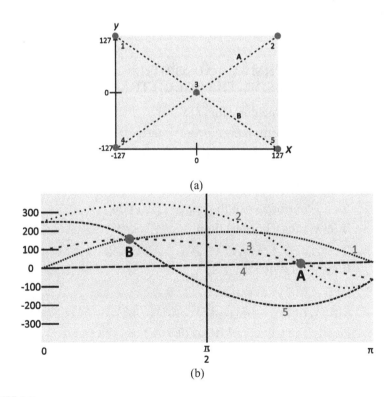

FIGURE 6.8
Partial results obtained from the application of the Hough algorithm for line detection in a simple image. (a) Original image and (b) the matrix of the accumulator records of the Hough parameter space.

where:

$$r\sqrt{\left(\frac{M}{2}\right)^2 + \left(\frac{N}{2}\right)^2}_{\text{max}} \qquad (6.9)$$

where M and N represent the width and height of the image.

6.3 Hough Transform Implementation

Algorithm 6.1 shows the way in which the parameters of the lines present in an image are found by means of the Hough Transform, using the one shown in Equation 6.6 as the straight-line model. A binary image is used as input to the algorithm, which contains edge information (extracted using methods such as those explained in Chapter 3). From now on, it will be used as a convention that a one in the image determines that the pixel is part of the border and a zero that it is part of the background.

ALGORITHM 6.1. ALGORITHM TO DETECT LINES USING THE HOUGH TRANSFORM.

Hough Transform line detector $\left(I(x,y)\right)$
MRAcc(θ, r) $\rightarrow$ Acummulation records matrix
$(x_c, y_c) \rightarrow$ Coordinates of the center of $I(x,y)$

1:      $0 \rightarrow$ **MRAcc(θ,r)**
2:      **for** all coordinates of the image $I(x,y)$ **do**
3:        **if** $(I(x,y)$ is a border) **then**
4:        $(x - x_c, y - y_c) \rightarrow (u,v)$
5:        **for** $\theta_i = 0...\pi$ **do**
6:        $r = u \cdot \cos(\theta_i) + v \cdot \sin(\theta_i)$
7:        **MRAcc(θ, r)** is increased.
8:        Finally, the registers **MRAcc(θ, r)** whose values are maximum are found.

As a first step, all the cells of the accumulation register matrix are set to zero (statement 1). Then the binary image is traversed (sentence 3) $I(x,y)$, in such a way that each time an edge pixel is found (that is, its value is one), the

values of r are obtained from Equation 6.6, performing a sweep of the parameter θ. from 0 to sentences 5 and 6). However, to find the values of r, the
center (x_c, y_c) of the image $I(x,y)$ is used as reference coordinates. For each
pair (r,θ) obtained from the scan, the register of the accumulation matrix is
increased (statement 7) by the indices corresponding to r and θ. In this way,
once all the pixels of the image have been traversed, the registers that have
been increased, obtaining the local maxima (sentence 8) that will correspond
to the values of (r,θ) that will define the lines identified in the image. $I(x,y)$.
In order to find the local maxima of the accumulator record matrix, a threshold is first applied so that only the points greater than that threshold remain,
and then a search is performed on the image, finding the local maxima found
in the image. considering a given neighborhood. The fact that the values of
several registers neighboring the register with the maximum value, whose
indices r and θ represent the parameters that model the real line contained in
$I(x,y)$, have large values, is due to the noise and inaccuracies produced by a
faulty quantization of the Hough parameter space.

Figure 6.9 shows a series of images that represent the partial results of
Algorithm 6.1. Figure 6.9a represents the original image produced artificially
to exemplify the use of Hough's algorithm for line detection. Figure 6.9b
shows the edges obtained by applying Canny's algorithm (see Chapter 7).
In Figure 6.9c, the content of the accumulation records matrix of the image is
shown. It can also be observed that the bright points represent those locations
whose values have increased significantly, becoming highly potential points
of the real parameters r and θ that represent the real lines of the original
image $I(x,y)$. Figure 6.9d shows the image produced by applying a threshold
to the accumulation records matrix. Figure 6.9e locates the records that have
a maximum value considering a given neighborhood. Finally, Figure 6.9f
shows the lines found using the Hough algorithm with parameters r and θ.

In Figure 6.9e, it can be seen from the maximum points obtained that the
closest points (5 and 6), practically contiguous, represent the parallel lines of
Figure 6.9a that have the same slope, that is, the same value of θ.

6.4 Encoding the Hough Transform in MATLAB

In this section, the Hough transform is implemented in the detection of lines
using MATLAB® as a programming language; however, it is worth men-
tioning that the tools already implemented in MATLAB that allow directly
detecting the lines in the image by means of the Hough transform are not
used in this section.

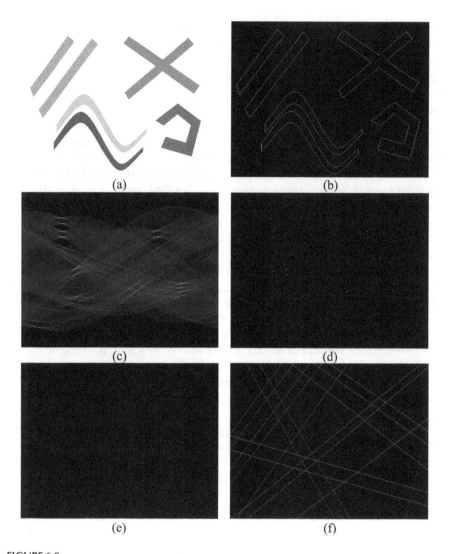

FIGURE 6.9
Partial results obtained from the application of the Hough algorithm for line detection in a real image. (a) Original image, (b) the edges of the original image, (c) the matrix of the accumulator records of the Hough parameter space, (d) image obtained from the application of the threshold to (c), (e) location of the maximum points, and (f) lines obtained by the application of the Hough algorithm.

For the implementation of the Hough transform, it is necessary to consider 3 different parts of the code. Program 6.1 shows the commented code that implements the Hough transform used for line detection.

PROGRAM 6.1. IMPLEMENTATION IN MATLAB OF THE HOUGH TRANSFORM

```
clear all
close all
I=imread('lineas.jpg');
I1=rgb2gray(I);
figure; imshow(I1)
%The edges of the image are obtained using the Sobel
method
BW=edge(I1,'Sobel');
figure, imshow(BW)
%The dimensions of the BW binary image are obtained
%where the pixels that have the value of 1 are part of
the border,
%while zero would mean that they are part of the
background.
[m,n]=size(BW);
%PART 1 (MRAcc is obtained)
%Some participating arrays are initialized
%in processing.
%The accumulation records matrix is initialized
MRAcc=zeros(m,n);
%The matrix where maximum locals obtained are stored
%is initialized
Fin=zeros(m,n);

%The center of the image is defined as
%a coordinate reference
m2=m/2;
n2=n/2;
%The maximum value of r is calculated depending on
%the dimensions of the image (see equation 8.9).
rmax=round(sqrt(m2*m2+n2*n2));
%The linear scaling of the
%Hough, Tetha and r parameters is obtained.
iA=pi/n;
ir=(2*rmax)/m;
%The BW image is traversed paying attention
%to the edge points where BW is one.

for re=1:m
  for co=1:n
    if(BW(re,co))
      for an=1:n
            %The center of the image is
            %considered a reference.
            x=co-n2;
```

```
            y=re-m2;
            theta=an*iA;
           %we obtain the value of r from 6.6
            r=round(((x*cos(theta)+y*sin(theta))/ir)+m2);
            if((r>=0)&&(r<=m))
           %The cell corresponding to the parameters
           %r and theta is increased by one
            MRAcc(r,an)= MRAcc(r,an)+1;
         end
       end
     end
   end
end
%PART 2 (The maximum record is selected locally)
%The MRAcc pixels are segmented by applying 100
%as threshold (th). In this way, the Flag pixels
%that are one will represent those records that
%constitute lines made up of at least 100 points.
%Accumulation record matrix is displayed
figure, imshow(mat2gray(MRAcc))
Bandera=MRAcc>100;
%The image is displayed after applying the determined
threshold
figure, imshow(Bandera)
%A neighborhood of 10 pixels is established
%for the search of the maximum.
pixel=10;
%The image is swept in search of the
%potential points
for re=1:m
  for co=1:n
    if(Bandera(re,co))
       %The search neighborhood
       %region is set
       I1=[re-pixel 1];
       I2=[re+pixel m];
       I3=[co-pixel 1];
       I4=[co+pixel n];
       datxi=max(I1);
       datxs=min(I2);
       datyi=max(I3);
       datys=min(I4);
       Bloc=MRAcc(datxi:1:datxs,datyi:1:datys);
       MaxB=max(max(Bloc));
       %The pixel of maximum value contained
       %in that neighborhood is selected.
       if(MRAcc(re,co)>=MaxB)
          %The maximum value pixel is marked
```

```
        %in the Fin array.
        Fin(re,co)=255;
      end
    end
    end
end
%The image is shown with the maximum points
figure, imshow(Fin)
%The coordinates of the pixels whose value
%was the maximum, which represented the records,
%whose indices represent the parameters of
%the detected lines, are obtained.
[dx,dy]=find(Fin);
%PART 3 (The lines found are displayed).
%The number of lines detected is
%obtained in indx, which implies the number
%of Fin elements.
[indx,nada]=size(dx);
rm=m;
cn=n;
apunta=1;
%The matrix M where the lines found will be
%displayed is initialized to zero
M=zeros(rm,cn);
%All lines found are displayed
for dat=1:indx
%The values of the parameters of
%the lines found are retrieved
pr=dx(dat);
pa=dy(dat);
%It is considered that the values
%of the parameters are defined considering
%the center of the image
re2=round(rm/2);
co2=round(cn/2);
%The values of r and theta are scaled
pvr=(pr-re2)*ir;
pva=pa*(pi/cn);
%The vertical and horizontal projections
%of r are obtained, since r is the vector
%defined at the origin and perpendicular
%to the detected line
x=round(pvr*cos(pva));
y=round(pvr*sin(pva));
%The offset considered is eliminated
%by using the center of the image as a reference
Ptx(apunta)=x+co2;
Pty(apunta)=y+re2;
```

```
%The considered index is increased to
%point to the parameters found that
%define the number of lines
apunta=apunta+1;
%The straight line model is scanned with
%the parameters detected and stored in
%the accumulator records matrix.
%First in one direction.
for c=x:1:co2
        r=round((-1*(x/y)*c)+y+(x*x/y))+re2;
        if((r>0)&&(r<rm))
            M(r,c+co2)=1;
    end
end
MRAcc=mat2gray(MRAcc);

%then in the direction not considered.
for c=x:-1:1-co2
    r=round((-1*(x/y)*c)+y+(x*x/y))+re2;
    if((r>0)&&(r<rm))
        M(r,c+co2)=1;
    end
end
end
%display of found lines
figure, imshow(M)
```

In the first part, in addition to initializing some variables, the Hough transform indicated by steps 1–7 of Algorithm 6.1 is implemented.

The second part of Program 8.1 is made up of the necessary instructions for choosing the pixels whose value of **MRAcc** is maximum within a block considered as the neighborhood region. To program such an event, the matrix (to which the threshold t_h was applied) is traversed sequentially, pixel by pixel, finding the maximum value of a neighborhood block or region $R(x,y)$ established around the point in question. To do this, the limits of the block relative to the pixel in question are set. In the case of Program 6.1, the interval is set equal to 10, which, considering it in both directions, would be 20. Once the limits are established, the block is extracted and the maximum is found. If the maximum of the block corresponds to the central pixel of the block relative to that of the scanning process, a one is placed in that position in the End matrix in such a way that the indices where there are ones in End will correspond to the parameters that define the lines of the original image. Figure 6.10 shows the process of finding the maximum within the considered neighborhood around the point in question.

In the third part, the straight lines found by applying the Hough Transform are displayed. For this, it is considered that the values of the parameters r

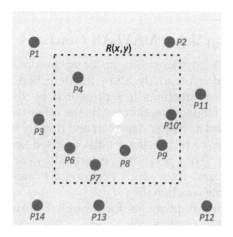

FIGURE 6.10
Process for obtaining the register of significant accumulators. Of all the points found by applying the threshold t_h, the one whose value **MRAcc** is the maximum in a defined neighborhood $R(x,y)$, is selected. In this case, the point value P5 has the maximum value of **MRAcc** compared to the other values P4, P6, P7, P8, P9, and P10 that are within the neighborhood region defined by $R(x,y)$.

and θ represent the vector that is perpendicular to the straight line that represents the one detected in the parameter space of the image. To formulate the model of the line to display, the only thing to consider is that if the slope of the vector is defined by $m = p_y/p_x$, considering that p_y and p_x are its vertical and horizontal projection, respectively, the slope of the line detected, which is the normal to this vector, will be the inverse and opposite to that of the vector $\left(-p_x/p_y\right)$. Figure 6.11 shows an illustration of this process.

It is important to mention that the images contained in Figure 6.9 were obtained by executing Program 6.1, in which what is described by the code can be observed graphically.

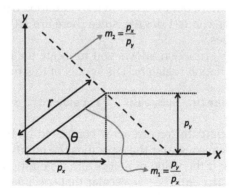

FIGURE 6.11
Slope of the detected line, which is the inverse and opposite to that of the vector defined by the parameters of the Hough Transform.

6.5 Line Detection Using MATLAB Functions

MATLAB contains 3 functions: hough, houghpeaks, and houghlines, which, when applied sequentially, allow the detection of lines in an image [7]. The core of these functions is represented by the Hough transform implemented in the Hough function, while the other two houghpeaks and houghlines are used as helper detection and display functions.

As explained, this set of functions must be used sequentially for a line detection application. The operations performed by each of these functions correspond to the parts into which Program 6.1 was divided, coding in MATLAB for the same functionality.

The hough function implements the Hough Transform, generating the array of accumulation registers; the houghpeaks function determines the registers whose maximum value defines the parameters of the detected lines; and finally, the houghlines function allows displaying the lines found by the combination of the hough and houghpeaks functions.

The hough function allows calculating the Hough Transform on a binary image that, as a prerequisite, contains the edges of an image. The syntax of this function is:

```
[H, theta, rho] = hough(BW);
```

where BW is a binary image containing the edges. The function returns 3 different values that are H, which contains the array of accumulator registers, and two vectors theta and rho that contain information on how linearly the parameters r and θ were divided in the array of accumulator registers of H.

When the Hough function is used with the syntax shown, it linearly divides the parameters r and θ, into 1997 values for the parameter r and 180 for the value of θ. So, the size of the accumulation records matrix will be 1997 × 180. The resolution of rho depends, as shown in Equation 6.9, on the size of the image, while that of rho is 1 degree, since there are 180 different indices to represent 180 degrees.

The houghpeaks function allows you to locate the maximum values of the array of accumulation registers. The syntax of this function is:

```
peaks = houghpeaks(H, numpeaks, 'Threshold', val);
```

where H is the accumulator record array computed by the hough function. The value numpeaks is a scalar that specifies the number of maximum values to identify in H. If the value of numpeaks is omitted in the syntax, the default value is 1. 'Threshold' is a scalar that specifies the threshold from which the H values are considered maximum. A simple way to determine a threshold that is correct and suitable for the accumulation record array is to use a proportional part of the maximum value found. An example is represented by the expression 0.5*max(H(:)), which implies that the defined threshold is 50% of the maximum value register.

The function houghpeaks obtains as a result a matrix of dimensions $Q\times2$, where Q is a value from 0 to numpeaks (maximum value to identify) and 2 implies the indices corresponding to the parameters r and θ that define the accumulator register found as maximum.

The houghlines function extracts the lines associated with the BW image calculated by the Hough Transform, implemented from the combination of the hough and houghpeaks functions. The syntax of this function is defined by:

```
lines = houghlines(BW, theta, rho, peaks);
```

where BW is the binary image in which the lines were detected through the Hough Transform, theta and rho are the vectors that define the way in which the accumulating records matrix was linearly divided and, at the same time, both calculated by the function hough. On the other hand, peaks is a matrix that was calculated by the houghpeaks function of dimension $Q\times2$, where Q is the number of lines detected and 2 are the indices corresponding to the parameters r and θ.

The houghlines function returns, as a result, an array of structures called lines. A structure is a grouping of data of different types under the same name. These data are called fields and are accessed using the format:

```
Name_of_the_structure.field1=3;
```

So, in the example above, field1, part of the structure Name_of_the_structure was assigned the value of 3. An array of structures is a set of index-driven structures that can be accessed using the format

```
Name_of_the_structure(1).field1=3;
```

where the value in parentheses refers to a structure identified by index 1.

The fields that the lines structure has are point1, point2, theta, and rho. Their meanings are summarized in Table 6.2.

6.5.1 Example of Line Detection Using MATLAB Functions

At the end of this section, an example is established that integrates the way in which the functions of the MATLAB image processing toolbox, described above, are used for the detection of lines in an image.

Considering as image Im to which it is desired to extract its lines as the one shown in Figure 6.12a, its edges are extracted by applying the function:

```
BW = edge(Im,'canny',0.1,0.1);
```

Resulting in image 6.12b. In this image, the Hough transform is applied by executing the function:

 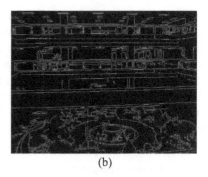

(a)   (b)

FIGURE 6.12
Detected lines by using the Hough transform method. (a) original image and (b) detected lines.

```
[H, theta, rho] = hough(BW);
```

To be able to graph the array of accumulation registers H, we will first have to convert this array from type double to type uint8, writing:

```
Hu=uint8(H);
```

to then make the graph by executing the following sequence:

```
imshow(Hu,[],'XData',theta,'YData',rho,'InitialMagnification',
'fit');
```

where the values of the 'XData' and 'YData' parameters replace the normal indices of the Hu matrix and the combination of the 'InitialMagnification' and 'fit' parameters allow the full-scale image of the window containing the graph to be displayed. The result is shown in Figure 6.13. You can also improve the deployment by using the command:

```
axis on, axis normal
```

by applying the function:

```
P = houghpeaks(H,8,'threshold',ceil(0.3*max(H(:))));
```

At most, the 8 points with the highest value of the accumulation record matrix H are obtained, considering 30% of the maximum value found as the threshold. In order to display the maximum points found in the accumulation matrix, the following command sequence is executed:

```
hold on

x = theta(P(:,2));
y = rho(P(:,1));
plot(x,y,'s');
```

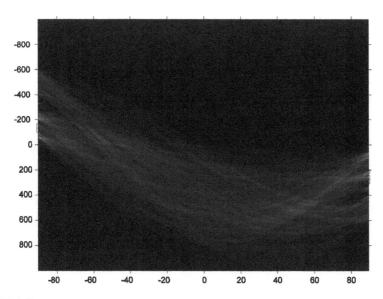

FIGURE 6.13
The matrix of the accumulator records of the Hough parameter space corresponding to the original image of Figure 6.12(a)

which allows retaining the image to place objects on it and obtain the vectors of the x and y coordinates of the maximum points. The image obtained by the previous sequence is shown in Figure 6.13.

Lastly, the lines corresponding to those of the parameters found by means of the houghlines function are obtained. However, since placing all the found line segments presupposes doing so by a repeat method, an .m file is programmed that allows finding the line segments and displaying the lines one by one on the BW border image. The .m file is shown encoded in Program 6.2 (Figure 6.14).

**PROGRAM 6.2.   PROGRAM TO FIND THE
LINE SEGMENTS AND DISPLAY THE LINES
ONE BY ONE ON THE BW EDGE IMAGE**

```
%%%%%%%%%%%%%%%%%%%%%%%%%%%%%%%%%%%%%%%%%%%%%%%%%%%%%%%%
%%%%
% Program that displays the lines calculated by the
functions
% hough, houghpeaks, houghlines over BW
```

```
%%%%%%%%%%%%%%%%%%%%%%%%%%%%%%%%%%%%%%%%%%%%%%%%%%%%%%%%%%%%%
%%%%
clear all
I=imread('fig9-14.jpg');
I1=rgb2gray(I);
BW=edge(I1,'canny',0.1,0.1);
[H, theta, rho]=hough(BW);
Hu=uint8(H);
imshow(Hu,[],'XData',theta,'YData',rho,'InitialMagnificat
ion','fit')
axis on, axis normal
P=houghpeaks(H,8,'threshold',ceil(0.3*max(H(:))));
hold on
x=theta(P(:,2));
y=rho(P(:,1));
plot(x,y,'s');
lines = houghlines(BW,theta,rho,P);
figure
imshow(BW);
hold on
max_len = 0;
%Arrays of structures found lines that contain the
%values of the lines are swept
for k = 1:length(lines)
xy = [lines(k).point1; lines(k).point2];
plot(xy(:,1),xy(:,2),'LineWidth',2,'Color','green');
%The start and end of the lines are plotted
plot(xy(1,1),xy(1,2),'x','LineWidth',2,'Color','yellow');
plot(xy(2,1),xy(2,2),'x','LineWidth',2,'Color','red');
%Determine the end of the longest segment
len = norm(lines(k).point1 - lines(k).point2);
if ( len > max_len)
    max_len = len;
xy_long = xy;
end
end
%Long segments are highlighted
plot(xy_long(:,1),xy_long(:,2),'LineWidth',2,'Color',
'cyan');
```

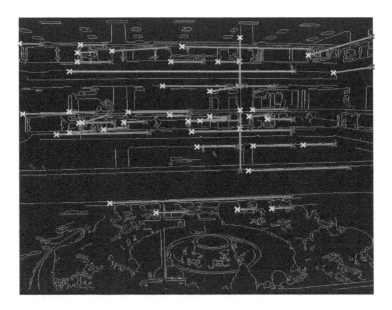

FIGURE 6.14
Image of edges, on which the line segments found by the combination of the hough, houghpeaks, and houghlines functions are placed. For the display of the lines, the code shown in Program 6.2 was used.

References

[1] Duan, D., Xie, M., Mo, Q., Han, Z., & Wan, Y. (2010). An improved Hough transform for line detection. In *2010 International Conference on Computer Application and System Modeling (ICCASM 2010)* (Vol. 2, pp. V2–354). IEEE.

[2] Illingworth, J., & Kittler, J. (1988). A survey of the Hough transform. *Computer vision, graphics, and image processing*, 44(1), 87–116.

[3] Kiryati, N., Eldar, Y., & Bruckstein, A. M. (1991). A probabilistic Hough transform. *Pattern Recognition*, 24(4), 303–316.

[4] Ballard, D. H. (1981). Generalizing the Hough transform to detect arbitrary shapes. *Pattern Recognition*, 13(2), 111–122.

[5] Hassanein, A. S., Mohammad, S., Sameer, M., & Ragab, M. E. (2015). A survey on Hough transform, theory, techniques and applications. *arXiv preprint arXiv*:1502.02160.

[6] Russ, J. C. (2011). *The image processing handbook* (6th ed.). CRC Press.

[7] McAndrew, A. (2017). *Introduction to digital image processing with MATLAB*. CRC Press.

Index

Note: *Italic* page numbers refer to figures.